W9-BZY-714

GROVE PRESS MODERN DRAMATISTS

Grove Press Modern Dramatists

Series Editors: *Bruce King* and *Adele King*

Published titles

Neil Carson, *Arthur Miller*

Ruby Cohn, *New American Dramatists, 1960–1980*

Bernard F. Dukore, *Harold Pinter*

Julian Hilton, *Georg Büchner*

Leonard C. Pronko, *Eugène Labiche and Georges Feydeau*

Theodore Shank, *American Alternative Theater*

Further titles in preparation

GROVE PRESS MODERN DRAMATISTS

HAROLD PINTER

by **Bernard F. Dukore**

Professor of Drama and Theater
University of Hawaii

Grove Press, Inc., New York

First published 1982 by The Macmillan Press Ltd.,
London and Basingstoke.

First Evergreen Edition 1982
First Printing 1982
ISBN: 0–394–17964–1
Library of Congress Catalog Card Number: 81–84705

Printed in Hong Kong

GROVE PRESS, INC., 196 West Houston Street, New York, N.Y. 10014

Contents

List of Plates

Editors' Preface

The *Grove Press Modern Dramatists* is an international series of introductions to major and significant nineteenth and twentieth century dramatists, movements and new forms of drama in Europe, Great Britain, America and new nations such as Nigeria and Trinidad. Besides new studies of great and influential dramatists of the past, the series includes volumes on contemporary authors, recent trends in the theatre and on many dramatists, such as writers of farce, who have created theatre 'classics' while being neglected by literary criticism. The volumes in the series devoted to individual dramatists include a biography, a survey of the plays, and detailed analysis of the most significant plays, along with discussion, where relevant, of the political, social, historical and theatrical context. The authors of the volumes, who are involved with theatre as playwrights, directors, actors, teachers and critics, are concerned with the plays as theatre and discuss such matters as performance, character interpretation and staging, along with themes and contexts.

vii

Editors' Preface

Grove Press Modern Dramatists are written for people interested in modern theatre who prefer concise, intelligent studies of drama and dramatists, without jargon and an excess of footnotes.

BRUCE KING
ADELE KING

Prefatory Notes

Except as indicated, quotations of Harold Pinter's works are from the three volumes titled *Collected Works*, published with the same pagination by Eyre Methuen in London and Grove Press in New York; these are cited parenthetically in the text by volume and page number. Quotations from *Old Times, No Man's Land*, and *Betrayal* are from the editions of the individual plays, published with the same pagination by the same firms; these are cited parenthetically in the text solely by page numbers, as are quotations from *The Hothouse*, published by Eyre Methuen in London and by Grove Press in the United States. Quotations from the short *Monologue* are from the Covent Garden Press edition (London), which lacks page numbers; now published by Eyre Methuen in London and by Grove Press in the United States. Other quotations of Pinter are cited in the usual manner at the end of the book.

Chapter 2 derives chiefly from the first chapter of Martin Esslin, *Pinter: A Study of His Plays*. I have augmented Esslin's chronology with the first chapter and appendix of

Prefatory Note

William Baker and Stephen Ely Tabachnick, *Harold Pinter*, the chronology that prefaces each volume of *Collected Works*, production information that introduces texts of individual plays, theatre programmes, newspaper indices, and the like. In chapter 2, only information from other sources is cited in footnotes.

For these and other works, the Bibliography provides full citations. It divides into two sections: Pinter's writings and selected secondary sources.

Because Pinter uses three dots to indicate a short pause, I enclose them within brackets to indicate ellipses.

1
Introduction

The changing response of many reviewers, spectators, and readers to Harold Pinter's plays recalls the familiar phrase 'Ontogeny recapitulates phylogeny' – that is, the development of the individual repeats the principal stages of the development of the group. Early in his career, audiences were mystified. When *The Birthday Party* opened in London, the unsigned reviewer of *The Manchester Guardian*, in a typical notice, dismissed Pinter as a writer of 'half-gibberish', whose characters 'are unable to explain their actions, thoughts, or feelings'; Milton Shulman of the *Evening Standard*, also typically, complained that witnessing this play resembled an attempt 'to solve a crossword puzzle where every vertical clue is designed to put you off the horizontal', and he predicted, 'It will be best enjoyed by those who believe that obscurity is its own reward.'[1] When *The Birthday Party* opened in the United States, a friend who attended the theatre with me raised similar objections and was annoyed that she, who had studied drama, could make no sense of the play; she was upset with her husband,

1

who lacking the dubious benefits of a university education decided, when he could not understand actions and speeches, that he would simply relax and enjoy the production; and she was irritated by me because, while I could not explain the play either to her or to myself, it created so riveting a world of its own, with a distinctive theatrical idiom, that I resolved to return to the theatre at the earliest opportunity – which I did, twice. Since this experience, twenty years ago, the lady has seen other plays by Pinter, finds no reason for incomprehension, and laughs at her initial response to *The Birthday Party*. Now, critical consensus on both sides of the Atlantic ranks Pinter among the best dramatists of our time. Between 1958 in London, or 1960 in San Francisco, and today, reviewers, spectators, and readers who have 'grown up with Pinter', as it were, have become accustomed to his dramatic stratagems. While some remain baffled by each new play, the difference between now and twenty years ago seems to be that mystification no longer matters. Other dramatic and theatrical factors occupy and absorb their attention. However, the experience of such middle-aged theatregoers and playreaders offers little comfort to those who come upon Pinter for the first time. Often they experience the same responses that people did in 1958 and 1960. Ontogeny recapitulates phylogeny.

This book is addressed to Pinter's new spectators and readers who feel puzzled and disoriented, and to those older ones who, while absorbed, remain mystified. It makes no attempt to explain the meanings of his plays. Rather it aims to explore Pinter's dramatic and theatrical stratagems which provide ways of enjoying and appreciating his plays, thus of understanding them, albeit in a non-explicatory manner.

To begin with I would like to introduce the characteristics, fascination, and difficulties of an encounter with Pinter via sets of quotations from his plays.

She places bacon and eggs on a plate, turns off the gas and takes the plate to the table. [. . .] *She returns to the stove and pours water from the kettle into the teapot, turns off the gas and brings the teapot to the table, pours salt and sauce on the plate and cuts two slices of bread.* BERT *begins to eat.* [. . .] *She butters the bread.* [. . .] *She goes to the sink, wipes a cup and saucer and brings them to the table.*

The Room (I,101)

(*indicating the sink*) What about this?
I think that'll fit in under here as well.
I'll give you a hand (*They lift it.*) It's a ton weight, en't?
Under here.
This in use at all, then?
No. I'll be getting rid of it. Here.
They place the sink under the bed.
There's a lavatory down the landing. It's got a sink in there.

The Caretaker (II,27)

The background, of a sink, stove, etc., and a window, is dim.

Landscape (III,175)

Among the highlights of English theatre in mid-century was the 1956 premiere of John Osborne's *Look Back in Anger*. Its immediate effect was incalculable. It introduced a phrase to the language ('angry young man'); it dealt with such contemporary issues as the atomic age; it vividly portrayed working-class characters and disillusioned young people who lived in the grey new world of the welfare state and who realistically spoke in the idiom of their classes; it realistically depicted their milieu, including grubby furniture, ironing boards, and newspapers strewn on the floor; it became a rallying-point for the under-thirty generation; and it inspired young playwrights to portray similar people in a similar manner. Sometimes regarded as a 'kitchen sink' type of drama, *Look Back in Anger* posed an alternative to the theatre of middle-class drawing-rooms and the concerns of those who live there.

Pinter's early commentators tended to group his plays under the 'kitchen sink' rubric. Indeed an influential critic included Pinter with Osborne and Arnold Wesker in an article named after it. As he observed, and as the first two epigraphs demonstrate, 'it is remarkable how many of these plays contain a kitchen sink or some equivalent, and there are continual reminders of food.'[2] The properties of Pinter's first few plays include sinks, food, or both; and the language of their characters, mostly working-class, is naturalistic, as if tape-recorded, with mumbling, repetitiveness, poor grammar, incomplete sentences, *non sequiturs*, sudden shifts of subject matter, refusal or inability to leave a subject another character has left, and the like.

As Pinter developed, however, and as the last epigraph suggests, the naturalistic side of his art became less pronounced. Even early critics recognised that despite their surface naturalism his plays had links to the then-new Theatre of the Absurd. Other highlights of English theatre in mid-century were the London productions of Samuel Beckett's *Waiting for Godot* and Eugene Ionesco's *The Lesson* in 1955, and of Ionesco's *The Bald Prima Donna* (called *The Bald Soprano* in America) in 1956. These playwrights are the major practitioners of the Theatre of the Absurd. Explaining the term, Martin Esslin, who coined it, cites Ionesco's statement that the Absurd has no purpose. In this sense man's existence in the universe is absurd. 'Cut off from his religious, metaphysical, and transcendental roots', says Ionesco, 'man is lost; all his actions become senseless, absurd, useless.' The sensation of metaphysical anguish when confronted by the absurdity of the human condition is the chief theme of the Theatre of the Absurd, which avoids discursiveness in dramatising it. Instead Absurdist drama presents this theme – at times with apparent irrationality – in terms of concrete stage images.[3] Recognising Pinter's affinities to the Absurdists, some critics pointed to Kafka, Beckett, and Ionesco as influences.[4] While Pinter admitted his admiration of Beckett and Kafka, and called Beckett 'the best prose writer living', he said that he had not heard of Ionesco until after he had written his first few plays.[5]

As he hinted in 1961, the School of Osborne and the School of Beckett, so to speak, are not mutually exclusive: 'what goes on in my plays is realistic, but what I'm doing is not realism' (II,11). In so far as production is concerned, 'what goes on' determines the style, realism. Peter Hall, who has directed Pinter's plays for stage and film, discusses them in terms of realistic production.[6] Clive Donner and Joan Kemp-Welch, who have directed them for movies and television respectively, agree upon the need for a basically realistic approach to Pinter's drama.[7]

> You wouldn't understand my works. You wouldn't have the faintest idea of what they were about.
>
> *The Homecoming* (III,77)

> Understanding is so rare, so dear.   *The Lover* (II,190)

> But what does that *mean*? What does it *mean*?
>
> *No Man's Land* (92)

I've often wondered what 'mean' means.

Tea Party (III,115)

When one considers the question of what a play might mean, one usually has in mind a phrase that encapsulates a play's theme or moral – perhaps that hell consists of other people (Jean-Paul Sartre's *No Exit*) or that exploited workers should strike (Clifford Odets's *Waiting for Lefty*). While such summaries might be reductive, they are not essentially inaccurate. Yet these examples are discursive plays whose authors want audiences to understand their thematic purposes. By contrast, playwrights like Chekhov and Beckett do not underscore their themes. Deliberately Chekhov avoids injecting his voice into the play; he wants his characters to reveal themselves, not to tell audiences what to infer or to believe. Beckett too refuses to employ a spokesman. To understand the work of such dramatists – and understanding is indeed rare – differs from the ability to reduce their meanings to paraphrase. As the last epigraph suggests, the term 'mean' requires a different type of understanding.

Pinter does not consider himself obliged to inject a remedy or thematic summary in the final act 'simply because we have been brought up to expect, rain or sunshine, the last act "resolution". To supply an explicit moral tag to an evolving and compulsive dramatic image seems to be facile, impertinent and dishonest.' When a playwright supplies it, he adds, perhaps alluding to Milton Shulman's review of *The Birthday Party*, he provides 'not theatre but a crossword puzzle' (I,12).

Like Beckett and unlike Bernard Shaw, he tries to avoid commenting on the meanings of his plays. He does not consider it part of his job to help audiences to understand them. This does not mean he does not want their understanding. Rather he feels that understanding 'can only come through the work itself' and is 'entirely their own responsibility'.[8]

Discussion of a play's meaning may take the form of an allegorical interpretation. Terence Rattigan liked to tell about meeting Pinter after he saw *The Caretaker*, which he considered an allegory: 'It's the Old Testament God and the New Testament God, with the Caretaker as humanity – that's what it's about, isn't it?' Pinter disagreed: 'It's about two brothers and a caretaker.'[9] For Pinter, characters and dramatic context are particularised. He has never, he says, 'started a play from any kind of abstract idea or theory' or has regarded his characters 'as allegorical representations of any particular force, whatever that may mean'. One reason he discourages this line of inquiry is: 'When a character cannot be comfortably defined or understood in terms of the familiar, the tendency is to perch him on a symbolic shelf, out of harm's way' (I,10–11). The last quotation is crucial to an understanding of Pinter's dramaturgy. He aims to provide audiences with direct experiences, which is not possible when form and meaning can be comfortably separated.

To deal with the type of meaning embodied in his plays, one might bear in mind Samuel Beckett's description of James Joyce's work that was later to be called *Finnegans Wake*: 'Here form *is* content, content *is* form. [. . .] His writing is not *about* something; *it is that something itself*.'[10] Pinter's plays are not 'about' something; they embody that something in dramatic and theatrical form. Meaning inheres in the direct impact of what happens on stage, not in an explanatory character or discursive dialogue.

This is a straight show.
What do you mean?
No dancing or singing.
What do they do then?
They just talk.   *The Birthday Party* (I,23)

I can take nothing you say at face value. Every word you
speak is open to any number of different interpretations.
                                   The Caretaker (II,82)

I thought you knew.   *Betrayal* (38)

In other words, apart from the known and the unknown,
what else is there?   *The Homecoming* (III,68)

Pinter's characters just talk, but as the Clown in
Shakespeare's *Twelfth Night* says, 'words are grown so false
I am loath to prove reason with them' (III,i). One can take
little they say at face value. Pinter's characters may contra-
dict themselves; they may have more than one name; and
what they say is open to several interpretations. To state
that they fail to communicate is only sometimes accurate.
More often they refuse to. Fearing to expose or reveal
themselves, they use words as 'a violent, sly, anguished or
mocking smoke screen which keeps the other in its place'.
Pinter calls this smoke screen a 'stratagem to cover naked-
ness' (I,14–15). The stratagem is not invariably successful.

Apart from the unknown and the known – which Pinter's
audiences, like his characters, try to determine – there is
the partly known: what is hinted but unverified. According to Pinter it may be unverifiable as well, and one cannot
always satisfy a desire to bridge the gap between unknown
and known, or between false and true. As the first epigraph
demonstrates, Pinter's talk, unclear or clear, unknown or

known, is extremely funny. The gap between each set of antitheses, like the desire to bridge it, creates comedy, not lugubrious meditations.

I can't remember. *Night* (III,223)

Yes, I remember. But I'm never sure that what I remember is of to-day or of yesterday or of a long time ago. And then often it is only half things I remember, half things, beginnings of things.

Silence (III,214)

There are some things one remembers even though they may never have happened. There are things I remember which may never have happened but as I recall them so they take place. *Old Times* (31–2)

Although the unreliability of memory is a major theme of Pinter's later plays, it inheres in his earlier works as well and is one reason for the difficulty of verifying what a character says. In 1962, Pinter spoke of 'the immense difficulty, if not the impossibility, of verifying the past. I don't mean merely years ago, but yesterday, this morning. [. . .] A moment is sucked away and distorted, often even at the time of its birth.' If people share a common ground, 'it's more like quicksand', for they interpret experience differently (I,11–12). Nine years later, he remarked on the mistiness of memory: 'If you were asked to remember, you really cannot be sure of whom you met 20 years before. And in what circumstances.'[11] As in life, Pinter's characters either cannot remember, are uncertain of the accuracy of their memory, or recognise that whatever they recall is true mainly for the present, however false it may be for the past. While their memories are unverifiable guides to the past,

they create a dramatic present that affects others and that
audiences verify before their eyes.

> You're a quiet one.   *No Man's Land* (19)

> Listen. What silence. Is it always as silent?
> It's quite silent here, yes. Normally.
> *Pause.*   *Old Times* (19)

Framed by dialogue, and achieving their effects in relationship to words, are various types of silence. According
to Peter Hall there are differences between Pinter's three
dots, pauses, and silences. While three dots constitute 'a
very tiny hesitation', a pause 'is really a bridge between
where the audience thinks that you're this side of the river,
then when you speak again, you're on the other side. [. . .]
It's a gap, which retrospectively gets filled in.' Silence is
more extreme, 'a dead stop [. . .] where the confrontation
has become so extreme, there is nothing to be said until
either the temperature has gone down, or the temperature
has gone up, and then something quite new happens.'[12]
Possibly for this reason, Pinter says that his characters are
clearest to him in their silences (I,14).

> I don't know who you are.   *The Room* (I,123)

> Do I know you?
> You'll know me when you see me.
> Do you know me?   *The Collection* (II,126)

Occasionally, I believe I perceive a little of what you are
but that's pure accident. [. . .] It's nothing like an accident, it's deliberate, it's a joint pretence. [. . .] What you
are, or appear to be to me, or appear to be to you,

10

changes so quickly, so horrifyingly, I can't keep up with it and I'm damn sure you can't either. [. . .] You're the sum of so many reflections. How many reflections? Whose reflections? Is that what you consist of? What scum does the tide leave? What happens to the scum? When does it happen? [. . .] What have I seen, the scum or the essence?   *The Dwarfs* (II,112)

Who people are and whether one can truly perceive their essence are issues in several of Pinter's plays. When his characters attempt to explain themselves they fail to clarify. The more detail they employ, the less convincing they become. Each piece of information about background and motivation proves to be partial information and raises new issues. The problem is not that one questions their reality but that one fails to understand them – a failure that is the dramatic point. Pinter objects to 'the becauses of drama' and asks, 'What reason have we to suppose that life is so neat and tidy?'[13] Like most people, he points out, his characters are usually 'inexpressive, giving little away, unreliable, elusive, evasive, obstructive, unwilling' (I,13–14). When one recognises the more intense reality of such dramaturgy, consternation may become fascination. Not only does this reversal create greater realism, it also provides what either conventionally realistic or conventionally symbolic drama does not: direct impact upon spectators and readers who are in the positions of the characters.

This tactic underlies the response Pinter supposedly made to a woman who wrote him:

Dear Sir, I would be obliged if you would kindly explain to me the meaning of your play *The Birthday Party*. These are the points which I do not understand: 1. Who are the two men? 2. Where did Stanley come from? 3. Were they all supposed to be normal? You will appreciate that without the answers to my questions I cannot fully understand your play.

Pinter replied in kind:

Dear Madam, I would be obliged if you would kindly explain to me the meaning of your letter. These are the points which I do not understand: 1. Who are you? 2. Where do you come from? 3. Are you supposed to be normal? You will appreciate that without the answers to my questions I cannot fully understand your letter.[14]

Implicitly, Pinter answered the woman's questions. By responding to her in precisely the same terms in which she responded to his characters, he invited her to respond to his characters in the same terms in which he responded to a real human being.

What follows is an exploration of Pinter's dramatic art. Chapter 2 consists of a biographical survey of the man and his work. Chapters 3 to 7 analyse his plays, which are grouped under convenient rubrics that convey different stratagems and emphases rather than mutually exclusive themes. Each chapter summarises several works but dwells on one full-length play. In chapter 3, 'Menace and the Absurd', that play is *The Birthday Party*; in chapter 4, 'Toward Greater Realism', it is *The Caretaker*. Chapter 5, 'Struggles for Power', stresses *The Homecoming*. In chapter 6, 'Memory Plays', the focal play is *Old Times*; in chapter 7, 'Recapitulations and Fresh Starts', *Betrayal* is discussed. The concluding chapter examines the place of Pinter's plays in modern drama.

2
Biographical Survey

Harold Pinter was born on 10 October 1930 in Hackney, a working-class neighbourhood in London's East End. His parents, both Jewish, were Hyman and Frances Pinter. He spent his first nine years in Lower Clapton, a short walk from the school in Hackney Downs that he would later attend. In Germany and Italy during the 1930s, fascist governments took hold, and their racial policies, favoured by English fascists, threatened Jews in England.

At the start of England's war with Germany, in 1939, Pinter was evacuated, with other London children, to the country. After a year or so in Cornwall, unfamiliar terrain to a city boy, he returned to his parents in London, then left with his mother for an area closer to the city. On the day they returned, in 1944, the Germans staged a V-2 rocket attack – a searing experience. Rocket raids continued, but while the Pinters evacuated their home several times, it remained unburned. After the war, Pinter recalls, Sir Oswald Mosley's fascists 'were coming back to life in England'. If one were Jewish, as he was, or looked as if he

13

were a communist, as he was not – though carrying books, he says, seemed to be *prima facie* evidence for such a political belief – he might be accosted by a group of fascist thugs. 'I got into quite a few fights down there', says Pinter, who adds, 'There was a good deal of violence there, in those days.'[1]

From September 1942 until July 1948 he attended the all-boys Hackney Downs Grammar School. He particularly admired his English master, Joseph Brearly, who was devoted to theatre and who directed him as Macbeth and Romeo. In the Literature and Debating Society he spoke on politics, literature, theatre, and film, and he wrote poetry and essays for the school magazine. But he was keen on sports as well: football, sprinting (he equalled the school record for 100 yards and set a new record for 220 yards), and cricket (he was vice-captain of the school team and was cited for best individual performance). He still plays cricket, in a team that includes fellow-dramatist Tom Stoppard.[2]

In 1948 he received a London County Council grant to study acting at the Royal Academy of Dramatic Art. At RADA he felt uncomfortable with what he perceived to be the other students' greater sophistication. Pretending a nervous breakdown, he roamed the streets instead of attending classes. Soon he left RADA.

That year, on his eighteenth birthday, he became eligible for National Service in the armed forces, but he refused on the ground that he was a conscientious objector. Because his objection was moral rather than religious, he brought to the conscientious-objector tribunal not a rabbi or minister but a friend, who told the board that whereas he himself was going to enter the army, it would be a waste of time to try to persuade Pinter to change his mind. Although two tribunals rejected Pinter's application for deferment, he refused to go when called. Twice he appeared before magistrates, who might have sent him to prison; instead they fined him – first ten, then twenty, pounds.

In 1949 he discovered Samuel Beckett's writing: an extract from the novel *Watt*, published in *Irish Writing*. Enthralled, he read Beckett's novel *Murphy*, and when *Watt* was published in 1953, he read it too. Today his enthusiasm for Beckett is undiminished, and he sends Beckett copies of the final typescripts of his plays.

In August 1950 *Poetry London* published two of his poems, 'New Year in the Midlands' and 'Chandeliers and Shadows' – his first professional publications, included in his *Poems and Prose: 1949–1977*. Because of serious printer's errors in the former, *Poetry London* repeated it in November with two new poems, this time under the pen name Harold Pinta.

On 19 September 1950 he gave his first professional performance, in *Focus on Football Pools*, for BBC radio. His first professional Shakespearean role followed: Abergavenny in *Henry VIII* broadcast by the BBC on 9 February 1951. Pinter then entered the Central School of Speech and Drama as an acting student. In September he obtained his first professional stage work, with Anew McMaster's company, touring Ireland through Autumn 1952. In 1953 he appeared with Donald Wolfit in a season of classics at the King's Theatre, Hammersmith, where he met actress Vivien Merchant (*née* Ada Thomson). The next year he adopted the stage name David Baron. From 1954 to 1957, he played standard West End and Broadway comedies and mysteries in provincial repertory theatres, including Colchester, Torquay, and Bournemouth, where he met Vivien Merchant again. In 1956 they married.

During these years as an actor he wrote – not plays, but poetry and fiction, including a short story, 'The Black and

White', which he turned into a review sketch in 1959, and a novel, 'The Dwarfs', based on his youth in Hackney. This novel was the genesis of his play of the same title.

At a party in London, Pinter was ushered into a room where he saw two men. The small man talked while he prepared food for the other, a large lorry driver who had his cap on and did not speak a word. Struck by this encounter he told a friend – Henry Woolf, then a student in the Drama Department of Bristol University – that he would one day write a play based on the image of two such people in a room. While Pinter was performing in a repertory company in Torquay, Woolf telephoned him and asked for the play. The call prompted him to write it sooner than he otherwise might have. In four afternoons he composed his first play, *The Room*. On 15 May 1957, under Woolf's direction, it was premiered at Bristol. The performance was so successful that on 20 December Bristol's other drama school, connected to the Bristol Old Vic, gave it a new production and entered it in *The Sunday Times* student drama competition. One of the judges, Harold Hobson, then drama critic of *The Sunday Times,* was so impressed that he wrote about it. His notice prompted a young producer, Michael Codron, to ask Pinter if he had written other plays. Pinter gave him two other works written in 1957, *The Party* (changed to *The Birthday Party*) and *The Dumb Waiter*.

On 29 January 1958 Pinter's and Merchant's son Daniel was born. That day Codron gave Pinter a £50 option to produce *The Birthday Party*. On 28 April it opened at the Arts Theatre, Cambridge; on 19 May in London, at the Lyric Theatre, Hammersmith. All of the daily newspapers savaged it. Its last performance was on 24 May. Total box office receipts were £260 11s. 5d, more than half for opening night. The low was Thursday matinee when six people paid £2 9s. Such an experience, Pinter said many years later, 'is a good way of getting old in this profession'.[3]

In *The Sunday Times,* 25 May, after the play had closed, Harold Hobson, displaying his usual acumen, declared his willingness 'to risk whatever reputation I have' by stating that Pinter, 'on the evidence of this work, possesses the most original, disturbing and arresting talent in theatrical London'. Despite the poor initial reception of *The Birthday Party*, he predicted that Pinter and the play 'will be heard of again'.[4]

In January 1959 Pinter directed *The Birthday Party* in Birmingham. On 22 March 1960 it was shown by Associated Rediffusion-TV. Thus millions of television viewers saw a play that daily newspapers, less than two years earlier, had found too obscure and arty. On 27 July 1960 it opened at the Encore, the smaller of the two theatres of the now-defunct Actors' Workshop of San Francisco – Pinter's first professional production in the United States, preceding Broadway by seven years. On 18 June 1964 the Royal Shakespeare Company revived *The Birthday Party* in London. Pinter, who directed it, regarded the production as unsatisfactory and vowed, 'I'm not going to direct any of my plays again'.[5]

On 29 July 1959 the BBC broadcast *A Slight Ache*, which it had commissioned from Pinter who wrote it in 1958. A stage version opened at the Arts Theatre, London, 18 January 1961. Pinter wrote review sketches, more radio plays, and television plays. *One to Another* opened at the Lyric Theatre, Hammersmith, with two Pinter sketches, 'Trouble in the Works' and 'The Black and White'. On 23 September *Pieces of Eight* opened, with new sketches: 'Request Stop', 'Last to Go', 'Special Offer', and 'Getting Acquainted'. During February and March 1964 the BBC broadcast nine sketches, five previously unperformed: 'Applicant', 'That's Your Trouble', 'That's All', 'Interview', and 'Dialogue for Three'. In 1959 Pinter completed *A Night Out*, broadcast 1 March 1960. On 24 April it was televised. On 17 September 1961 a stage version opened at the Gate Theatre, Dublin; on 2 October at the Comedy Theatre, London. On 21 July 1961 *Night School* was televised. The BBC broadcast Pinter's radio play *The Dwarfs*, derived from his unpublished novel, on 2 December 1960. A stage version opened at the Arts Theatre, London, on 18 September 1963. *The Collection*, written for television, was shown on 11 May 1961. The Royal Shakespeare Company staged it at the Aldwych Theatre, London, on 18 June 1962.

Meanwhile, works originally written for the stage were produced in 1960. On 21 January a double bill of *The Room* and *The Dumb Waiter* opened at the Hampstead Theatre Club. On 27 April *The Caretaker* – Pinter's second full-length play, written in 1959 – opened at the Arts Theatre, London. His first major critical and popular success on the English stage, *The Caretaker*, transferred to the Duchess Theatre on 30 May to begin a year's run on the West End, and it received the 1960 *Evening Standard* Drama Award. On 4 October 1961 it opened in New York – his first Broadway production. A critical success, not a commercial one, it closed after four months.

The Caretaker was Pinter's first play to be filmed, adapted by the playwright and directed by Clive Donner. Shooting began on 12 December 1962 on location in Hackney, near his childhood home. In 1963 it opened in England; in 1964 in America, where it was called *The Guest* – probably because a Joan Crawford film, *The Caretakers*, had opened in 1963. Pinter's next play to be filmed was *The Birthday Party,* which opened in New York in 1968. Adapted by the author it was directed by William Friedkin (who would later direct *The French Connection* and *The Exorcist*).

After the *Caretaker* film Pinter began to write screen

adaptations of novels by other writers. *The Servant*, from Robin Maugham's work, was his first collaboration with director Joseph Losey. It opened in 1963. The next year his version of Penelope Mortimer's *The Pumpkin Eater* opened, directed by Jack Clayton (who had directed *Room at the Top*). In 1966 *The Quiller Memorandum*, based on Adam Hall's *The Berlin Memorandum*, and directed by Michael Anderson (who had directed *Around the World in Eighty Days*), was shown. *Accident*, adapted from Nicholas Mosley's novel, opened in 1967, directed by Losey. In 1969 Pinter adapted L. P. Hartley's *The Go-Between* for Losey; it opened in 1971. That year he wrote a screen version of Aidan Higgins's novel *Langrishe Go Down*, which has not yet been filmed. In early 1973 he completed another adaptation for Losey, *The Proust Screenplay*, based on *À la recherche du temps perdu*. Assisting him was Barbara Bray, a Proustian authority, who had directed *The Dwarfs* for BBC radio. Pinter published the screenplay which has not yet been filmed. In 1974 he adapted F. Scot Fitzgerald's *The Last Tycoon*. Directed by Elia Kazan (veteran of American stage and film, whose productions in both include *A Streetcar Named Desire*), it opened in 1976. In 1979 he adapted John Fowles's *The French Lieutenant's Woman*, directed by Karol Reisz (who had directed *Saturday Night and Sunday Morning*).

While adapting the works of others he continued to write his own, original plays. On 28 March 1963 *The Lover*, written in 1962, was televised. On 18 September, in tandem with *The Dwarfs* and directed by Pinter, it opened at the Arts Theatre, London. On 25 March 1965 the BBC televised *Tea Party*, written 1964, as part of a series, 'The Largest Theatre in the World', organised by the European Broadcasting Union which co-operated in commissioning works (from Terence Rattigan and Fritz Hochwälder, among others) and showing them simultaneously, or almost so, throughout Europe. On 28 February 1967 the BBC televised *The Basement*, originally written in 1963 as *The Compartment* for a project sponsored by Grove Press, the American publisher of Pinter, Beckett, and Ionesco.[6] It was to have been part of a trio of short films, with Beckett's *Film* and Ionesco's *The Hardboiled Egg*. To date only *Film* has been filmed. On 10 October 1968 *Tea Party* and *The Basement* had their stage premieres at the off-Broadway East Side Playhouse, New York, the first and, so far, only time Pinter's works have been produced on an American stage before an English one. On 17 September 1970 they opened at the Duchess Theatre, London.

Pinter's next major work for the stage was *The Homecoming*, written in 1964. On 3 June 1965 the Royal Shakespeare Company presented it at the Aldwych Theatre, London. A year later Pinter was named Commander of the Order of the British Empire in the Queen's Birthday Honours List. Wryly he emphasised that his CBE came 'The year *after* the Beatles' were similarly honoured.[7] On 3 January 1967 *The Homecoming* opened on Broadway. While it was not a commercial success, it received huge critical acclaim – including four 'Tonies' (Antoinette Perry awards) and the New York Drama Critics' Award – and decisively established Pinter's reputation in America. In 1973 the American Film Theatre version opened.

Although Pinter had not directed his own plays since 1964, he directed works by others: Robert Shaw's *The Man in the Glass Booth* (London, 1967; New York, 1968), Simon Gray's *Butley* (London, 1970; New York, 1971; American Film Theatre, 1973), James Joyce's *Exiles* (London, 1970), John Hopkins's *Next of Kin* (London, 1974) Gray's *Otherwise Engaged* (London, 1975; New York, 1976), Noel Coward's *Blithe Spirit* (London, 1976),

Gray's *The Rear Column* (London, 1978) and *Close of Play* (London, 1979).

In 1968 Pinter refused to make cuts or changes in *Landscape*, as demanded by the Lord Chamberlain in charge of stage censorship – the last year the English stage was so afflicted. The chief offending phrase was 'Fuck all', which Pinter would not amend to 'Bugger all' or something similarly innocuous. According to a possibly apocryphal story, Pinter – whose refusal to submit to National Service twenty years earlier would suggest a refusal to submit to censorship – gave a characteristically terse explanation for retaining the first word: 'I need a monosyllable'. Because the Lord Chamberlain's jurisdiction did not extend to radio, the BBC broadcast it, on 25 April, without cuts. Thus stage censorship resulted in the play reaching a far larger audience than any stage production would. In 1969 Pinter completed *Silence*. With the Lord Chamberlain's authority gone, the Royal Shakespeare Company produced it on 2 July in a double bill with *Landscape* at the Aldwych Theatre, London. In 1970 the Repertory Theatre of Lincoln Center, New York, produced them in its smaller house, the Forum.

On 1 June 1971 the RSC premiered *Old Times*, written in 1970, at the Aldwych. In November it had its Broadway premiere. On 13 April 1973 the BBC televised *Monologue*, written in 1972, a one-man play with Henry Woolf who had started Pinter on his playwriting career fifteen years before. On 3 December 1975 Pinter played the role on BBC radio.

His next full-length play was *No Man's Land*, written in 1974, produced by the National Theatre at the Old Vic on 23 April 1975. On 15 July it transferred to Wyndham's Theatre in the West End; the following year to Broadway. In 1977 Granada TV filmed it; it was televised in 1978.

In July 1975, while he was directing *Otherwise Engaged*

Vivien Merchant sued Pinter for divorce because he was otherwise engaged with Lady Antonia Fraser, popular biographer, wife of the Tory MP Hugh Fraser, and daughter of the Earl of Longford, whose anti-smut crusades brought him the nickname 'Lord Porn'. In December 1976 the Frasers were divorced. Vivien Merchant then withdrew her suit; but in August 1980, she and Pinter were divorced. On 9 October, Pinter and Lady Antonia announced that they were married. 'In suitably Pinteresque secrecy', as *The Times* put it, 'they would not say where or when the ceremony took place'.[8] In November, however, with equal suitability, certainty disappeared from Pinter's factual announcement. That month, it was discovered that Vivien Merchant had neglected to sign the divorce papers, thereby invalidating Pinter's new marriage. She then signed them, whereupon Pinter and Lady Antonia underwent a second marriage ceremony.

Betrayal opened in London on 15 November 1978 at the National Theatre's Lyttleton Theatre. Its Broadway premiere took place on 5 January 1980 and marks Pinter's first major commercial success in American theatre.

After writing *Betrayal*, he reread *The Hothouse*, written in Winter 1958. Then, he considered it too explicitly satiric and discarded it (save for one scene, used in the sketch 'Applicant'). Twenty-one years later he considered it stageworthy.[9] On 1 May 1980 it opened at the Hampstead Theatre Club. Pinter also reconsidered his resolution about directing his own work. He himself staged *The Hothouse*. As this book goes to press, his most recent play is *Family Voices*, which BBC Radio broadcast in January 1981. On 13 February, the National Theatre staged it at the Lyttleton Theatre.

3
Menace and the Absurd

In 1957 David Campton coined the term 'Comedies of Menace' as the subtitle of his one-act plays collectively called *The Lunatic View*. In 1958 Irving Wardle applied it to *The Birthday Party*. Although he subsequently wanted to withdraw the label,[1] its aptness made it stick.

'Comedies of Menace' puns on 'Comedies of Manners'. Like such comedies by Congreve and Shaw, Pinter's drama provokes laughter through balanced phraseology, antithesis, and the language and manners of social classes – though the classes in his plays are usually lower than those in Congreve's and Shaw's. Consider an exchange early in *The Birthday Party*: 'Is Stanley up yet?' 'I don't know. Is he?' 'I don't know. I haven't seen him down yet.' 'Well then, he can't be up' (1,20). The passage is rhythmic, with two stresses in each of the first two speeches, three in each of the last two, balancing each other and counterpointing 'up' with 'down'. This antithesis helps create comedy, as does the accurate reproduction of spoken English, with clichés,

23

repetitiveness, and incomplete understanding. Realism is the basis of much of Pinter's comedy, including *non sequitur*, as in this dialogue between Rose and Mr Kidd in *The Room*: 'Anyone live up there?' 'Up there? There was. Gone now.' 'How many floors you got in this house?' 'Floors. (*He laughs.*) Ah, we had a good few of them in the old days.' 'How many do you got now?' 'Well, to tell you the truth, I don't count them now' (I,108). The incongruity of old Kidd saying that the house used to have a goodly number of floors (implying it no longer does) and that he does not count them (implying he used to) is very funny. Yet his responses may be logical, for the old man might refer to the tenants upstairs, not floors.

Such comic passages also help create an atmosphere of menace, mystery, evasion, and matters deliberately concealed. Frequently Pinter's plays begin comically but turn to physical, psychological, or potential violence – sometimes, in varying sequences, to all three. Terror inheres in a statement in *The Room* that the onstage room, which is occupied, is to let. Although the play turns comic again, it ends on a note of physical violence.

In the early plays menace lurks outside, but it also has psychological roots. The titular room – in which the heroine lives, fearful of an outside force she does not specify – is dark. In *The Birthday Party* the sheltered young man fears visitors. In *The Dumb Waiter* outside forces menace a questioning killer. In *A Slight Ache* a psychologically disturbed man fears a man he invites inside. While menace may take the shape of particular characters, it is usually unspecified or unexplained – therefore, more ominous.

Partly because realistic explanations are absent, disturbing questions arise. One is unsure why characters visit others, why they commit inexplicable actions, why the others fear them. Frustrated reviewers or readers accuse Pinter of wilful obfuscation. Yet before he began to write plays, he had acted in conventional works with clear exposition and pat conclusions. The fact that his own, unconventional plays contain neither should alert one to the possibility that other dramatic aspects are more important, that Pinter's refusal to focus on answers to 'Who?' and 'Why?' is a deliberate effort to focus on answers to 'What?' and 'How?' To put the matter another way, present activities, interrelationships, and stratagems are more dramatically important than past actions. His drama is not a matter of They have been, therefore they are; but rather, They do, therefore they are.

These early plays conform to the characteristics of the Theatre of the Absurd, as explained in chapter 1. Their effective unsettling quality, with its fusion of realism and nonrealism, distinguishes Pinter's artistic signature from those of other writers of this genre. Because events and actions are unexplained, and apparently illogical or unmotivated, the world seems capricious or malevolent. One can rely upon nothing. What is apparently secure is not secure. A haven does not protect. A weapon vanishes without warning. Linguistic absurdity may suggest the absurdity of the human condition. Fear of a menace may suggest the universal trauma of man in the universe.

With such works as Georg Büchner's *Danton's Death*, Bernard Shaw's *Widowers' Houses*, and Bertolt Brecht's *Baal*, Harold Pinter's *The Room* ranks among the most astonishing first plays ever written. Like the authors of these earlier works, that of *The Room* speaks in a distinctive, resounding, authoritative, and compelling voice, employing themes and techniques his later plays would develop.

The Room begins with a dramatisation of Pinter's chance encounter at a party in London, alluded to earlier. In the play a woman talks while she prepares food for her husband, a silent van driver. Rose and Bert Hudd are interrupted by the landlord, Kidd, with whom she talks at cross-purposes. After he leaves, Bert goes for a run in his van. Soon she is interrupted by Mr and Mrs Sands who claim to be apartment-hunting. Seeking the landlord, they met, in the dark basement, a man who told them of a vacancy: the flat where Rose and Bert live. After the Sands depart, Kidd returns, pleading with Rose to receive the man in the basement who wants to see her alone. Kidd's earlier visit was to discover whether Bert had gone. The visitor is a blind Negro named Riley who tells Rose her father wants her to come home, and who calls her Sal. Bert returns to find them together. He knocks Riley to the floor, strikes him, and kicks his head against the stove until he lies still – possibly dead. Rose then cries out that she is blind.

A logical starting point for an examination of *The Room* is Pinter's statement, 'My plays are what the titles are about'.[2] So they are. To Rose, as she repeatedly insists, the room represents security from the world outside. However, it is not entirely safe. Despite its resemblance to rhyming alternatives, *The Room* differs from *The Tomb* which permits no exit, and *The Womb* which, permitting no entry, is entirely secure. Nor is *The Room* the same as *The Home*, which might suggest ownership or belonging.

What happens in the play involves what spectators see and hear (or what readers see in their mind's eye and hear in its ears). Insecurity and fear create dramatic tensions and account for many ambiguities, contradictions, and character interrelationships. Rose fears the basement, a subject she claims to be rid of but which frequently intrudes itself into monologue and dialogue. She talks of how warm the room is, but the cold forces her to wrap her cardigan about her; and though she insists no one bothers Bert and her in the room, the action demonstrates a succession of intruders who bother them.[3] Kidd rambles on about his family, yet he refuses to respond when Rose asks what his younger sister died of; after his departure she says she does not believe he had a sister.

What happens creates an atmosphere of suspicion and fear. Therefore ambiguities and contradictions are understandable, for people evade issues and refuse to reveal themselves. Such evasion and stealth are among the play's subjects. In other words it is not the characters' background that is of major dramatic concern but their avoidance of revealing it. Thus when Riley calls Rose 'Sal', she does not deny it is her name but tells him not to call her by it. Pinter could easily resolve the apparent contradiction, for both may be nicknames of Rosalie or she may have two given names, each used by different sets of acquaintances. What matters is that the different name frightens her.

As the start of this chapter indicates, *The Room* – fear notwithstanding – is frequently funny. Comedy derives from *non sequitur* (the passage on floors previously quoted), repetitive patter ('Well, that's not the bloke we're looking for', 'Well, you must be looking for someone else' (I,111)), and the fact that the woman jabbers for over four pages while the man does not utter a word (by the time she asks how he liked the rasher she served, one is unsurprised – and amused – when she answers the question herself).

Rose's opening monologue contains linguistic links to various scenes of the play. Sprinkled throughout it are comments about darkness, sight, blindness, and murder. Later Kidd employs an image of blindness and the Sands mention sight and darkness. Although there is no rational basis for Rose's sudden blindness, her verbal preoccupation with sight, darkness, and blindness suggests that she has an affinity to Riley – one that is buttressed by his message. Thus when Bert kicks and apparently kills him, her sudden blindness is like a transference between kindred spirits. Furthermore the imagery of murder and death anticipates the violence Bert perpetrates upon Riley. For this reason, perhaps, most commentators conclude that Riley dies, though Pinter's stage direction describes him only as inert. Also Rose's monologue at the opening is balanced by Bert's virtual monologue at the end (when Riley starts to interrupt, Bert strikes him). Such connectives and symmetry are among Pinter's dramaturgical trademarks. Through language and scenic balance he constructs emotional rather than rational links, by which he implies what he does not elucidate.

As in *The Room, The Birthday Party* has a character (this time, male) who fears intrusion from without. Instead of Riley, a blind Negro, entering to reclaim the person hiding, representatives of other minority groups come – a Jew and an Irish Catholic, though the Jew's speeches suggest conformity to the English mainstream and the Irishman, as one critic notes, sings a song about Reilly.[4] As before, the menace that visits the sequestered person suggests the absurdity of the human condition, for this man, like mankind, is unsafe and without certainties in his universe. Nonrealism mixes with realism. In *The Room* blindness transfers from one person to another; in *The Birthday Party* interrogation consists of rationally meaningless combinations of questions and accusations – also suggestive of the absurd.

Stanley Webber, a lodger in the house of Meg and Petey

Boles, in a seaside town, seems not to have left it since he arrived the year before. Goldberg and McCann arrive, brutally interrogate him, break his eyeglasses, crush his spirit, drive him to a breakdown – following which he cannot speak coherently – and take him away with them. Goldberg has an affair with Lulu, a neighbour, but he and McCann turn her away when her presence interrupts their activities with Stanley. Pinter does not reveal why Stanley is in the lodging house or why the intruders do what they do.

True to its title *The Birthday Party* contains a birthday party – for Stanley who insists it is not his birthday. Birthday not only means the anniversary of one's birth, it also means the day of one's birth, and in *The Birthday Party* the celebration of the former helps to create the latter. The intruders turn Stanley into what McCann calls a new man. At their hands he is reborn, made into a different kind of person on a birthday that becomes a birth-day.

What happens on stage is what the audience perceives, not the symbolic nature of actions or speeches. For instance McCann calmly tears a newspaper into five equal strips while Stanley nervously paces. To be sure one can interpret McCann's action as the destruction of a medium of communication, which it is, yet this interpretation reveals nothing essential about the play for communication is not a major theme. More important is that the action simultaneously calms McCann and unnerves Stanley.[5]

When Stanley hears of two visitors he apprehensively questions Meg about them, paces the room, and insists they will not come. Pinter does not explain why he is nervous. What matters is that he is nervous. When Goldberg and McCann arrive Stanley peeks at them through the kitchen serving-hatch and sneaks out through the rear door. Mystery and menace increase when McCann asks Goldberg if they are in the right house, for he saw no number on the gate. 'I wasn't looking for a number', says Goldberg (I,38). They intensify when Goldberg questions Meg about her lodger and, upon learning it is the lodger's birthday, decides – not impulsively but '*thoughtfully*' – that a party should celebrate the event. '*We're* going to give him a party' [author's italics] (I,42–3). No reason is offered. What matters is that Goldberg's decision is deliberative and that he immediately assumes command of the household. After he and McCann go to their rooms Stanley questions Meg about the newcomers. Upon hearing that one is named Goldberg he responds by slowly sitting at the table. When she asks if he knows them he does not reply – then or later. What the play shows is that their presence and Goldberg's name unsettle him.

Meg's first actions in relationship to Stanley are very funny. She calls to him, as she would to a child, to come down to breakfast; she races to his room, rousing him, while he shouts and she laughs wildly; finally he enters – not a boy, but a bespectacled, groggy man in his thirties, unshaven, and wearing his pyjama jacket. Underlying these activities, what is often called the subtext, is that someone makes Stanley do what he does not want to do – a comic foreshadowing of a noncomic resolution. Furthermore Stanley's comic dissatisfaction with his reward, breakfast, hints at a more disturbing dissatisfaction to come. This attempt to make someone go where he does not wish to go becomes a leitmotif. Meg suggests that Stanley go shopping with her; he refuses. Lulu urges him to go outside for a walk; he refuses. At the end he is forced to leave the house, not merely his room – a noncomic departure this time. Goldberg and McCann say they will take him to Monty but do not explain who Monty is or what he represents. That Pinter does not have them do so indicates that the specific reason for his removal is unimportant. The dramatic point is that they take him, in contrast to his going of his own volition. His removal, the theatrical climax of this leitmotif, resembles a symphonic finale of a musical theme, not a discursive explanation of a literary theme.

Present speech and action are more important than exposition. Stanley's references to his career as a pianist dwindle, both comically and pathetically, from giving concerts throughout the world to giving them all over the country to once giving a concert. Dramatically what matters is not which if any of these statements is true but that Stanley makes them in this sequence, for by doing so he verbally nonentitises himself. Later Meg further undercuts his status as a pianist when, after twice saying she enjoyed watching him play the piano, she repeats his story about the concert and (comically) gets the details wrong. She undercuts that status still further (again comically) when she gives him a toy drum as a birthday present – because he does not have a piano.

What happens on stage contributes to the audience's sense, feeling, or understanding. The passages that describe Stanley as a pianist convey the impression that he is an artist, an artist-manqué, or a parody of an artist. By contrast, partly because an artist is often regarded as one who does not conform to customary social roles and partly because Goldberg's conventional appearance contrasts with that of the unkempt Stanley, Goldberg suggests social conformity (he even carries a briefcase). His speeches sometimes seem to parody corporate jargon, at other times overflow with the clichés of middle-class conformity. In large measure he and McCann convey an ambience of conformity (family, state, and church) and appear as representatives of society who press Stanley into a mould. As if in summary they promise Stanley he will be adjusted. Appropriately they represent the two traditional religions of European civilisation, Judaism and Catholicism. For *Protest*ants to make Stanley conform would be inappropriate.

Pinter creates atmosphere by the theatrical nature of words: rhythms and quantity. When the visitors interrogate the lodger what they say is contradictory or illogical, but how they say it, and Stanley's inarticulateness or silence, have theatrical meaning. They accuse him of killing his wife and of not marrying, of not paying the rent and of contaminating womankind, of picking his nose and of being a traitor to the cloth. Stanley hardly has an opportunity to get a word in edgeways. Clearly the scene's effectiveness is unrelated to causal logic. As Glynne Wickham explains, 'Three characters are speaking in this interrogation episode, but the rhythmic structure is a single sequence. The horror of this remarkable scene, and its impact on the audience, is achieved by the deliberate antithesis of verbal *non sequitur* against the remorselessly mounting insistence of the verbal rhythm.'[6] In addition, according to one critic, impact and ambience derive not from the accuracy or relevance of any particular accusation but from 'the sheer weight, variety, and quantity of usage'.[7] Here language is used theatrically, not referentially, as it is in the duo's final scene with Stanley where a stage direction says, '*They begin to woo him, gently and with relish*' (I,92). In these speeches two voices speak with one rhythm.

Implicit in some of the previous analysis is the play's comedy which links to later sequences that are not comic. *The Birthday Party* begins with humour derived from incongruity and verbal repetition. After Meg thrice asks her husband whether it is he who has entered, he responds: 'What?' 'Is that you?' 'Yes, it's me.' 'What?' (I,19). The opening exchange of Act III balances that of Act I, but the later scene is not funny. Furthermore Meg is mistaken about the visitor: as in Act I Petey enters, but in Act III Meg asks if it is Stanley. Identity, the subject of both exchanges, is thematically relevant. In Act I Stanley asks Meg whether, when she addresses him, she knows exactly whom she talks to. In Act II he tells McCann he is the same as he has always been. In Act III, however, the intruders promise to change his identity.

In Act I comedy derives from food Meg offers Petey and Stanley: fried bread that Stanley mockingly calls succulent, milk he calls sour, and tea he compares to gravy. By contrast there is no food left for either in Act III, since the intruders have eaten everything. Food suggests sustenance, and there is none for Petey who is too feeble to resist the well-nourished Goldberg and McCann, or for Stanley who is incapable of resisting them. Apropos, when Stanley calls the bread succulent, Meg does not understand the meaning of the word which sounds sexual. As the comic misunderstanding demonstrates, a word's meaning is not necessarily referential; in the interrogation scene the rhythms not the meanings of words have a devastatingly noncomic effect on Stanley.

Anticipating later conflicts, the first act has Meg and Stanley engage in a minor, comic struggle for domination. When he requests tea she demands: 'Say please.' 'Please.' 'Say sorry first.' 'Sorry first' (I,27). His mockery suggests his victory. In the next act a battle for domination revolves around whether Stanley will sit as directed. The battle is comic, suggestive of a child's game, with I'll-sit-if-you-sit and Stanley rising immediately after Goldberg and

McCann sit. When Goldberg then rises, McCann reprimands Stanley and shouts at him to sit. Stanley tries to
appear casual by whistling and strolling, but he obeys. Next
the two menacingly interrogate him. Though the request to
sit is apparently as trivial as the request to say please, and
though it is initially as comic, what underlies both demands
– what happens – is that a person or persons make another
do what he does not want to do. The manoeuvre that is
comic foreshadows menace.

In *The Birthday Party* Pinter links the visual with the verbal. In Act I, for example, when Goldberg and McCann
meet Meg they say: 'How often do you meet someone it's a
pleasure to meet?' 'Never.' 'But today it's different. How
are you keeping, Mrs Boles?' (1,40). How might Meg
respond to Goldberg's first question? Is she pleased or does
the flattery pass her by? In either case how does she
respond to McCann's thoughtless answer? Does she understand its implications? Does Goldberg respond to it? The
answer to this determines how and to whom he says that
today is different. He might reassure Meg or he might reprimand his colleague, and the different possibilities determine his rendering of the next question. Whether one inter-
prets the brief exchange as two visitors hurrying the mistress of the house through a perfunctory introduction or as
a comic scene in which Goldberg finesses McCann's social
blunder, it is important to consider not only the dialogue
but also the relationship between the speakers and the
silent character. Visual links with verbal.

Directorial embellishments can visually fortify the verbal. Alan Schneider's Broadway production did so. Perhaps taking a cue from Goldberg's assertion that McCann is
a defrocked priest, Edward Winter (McCann), during the
scene in which he exhorts Lulu to confess, placed two strips

of torn newspaper over each of his shoulders as if they were a priest's vestment.

At the close of Act I the visual combines with nonverbal sound to create meaning: a climax of terror as Stanley, drum hanging from his neck, marches around the table beating the drum regularly, then erratically and uncontrolled, and when he arrives at Meg's chair his face and drumbeat are savage. At the climax of Act II the lights suddenly go out. From the darkness spectators hear groping for a torch, grunts from Goldberg and McCann, the sustained beating of a drumstick on a drum, whimpers from Lulu, people stumbling against each other, and dialogue – for a page and a half, a long time in the theatre. McCann finds the torch and shines it over the room until he picks out Stanley, bent over a spreadeagled Lulu. The light draws closer to him, he backs up against the serving-hatch, and he giggles as Goldberg and McCann converge upon him. Through theatrical elements, not discursive language, Pinter conveys Stanley's increasing breakdown.

When Stanley appears in the last act the very sight of him indicates the intruders' triumph and his conformity. No longer unkempt, as in Act I, he is as immaculate as a corpse and walks like a zombie. Clean-shaven, he wears a dark, well-tailored suit and white collar, and he holds his broken glasses. A stage direction has Goldberg easily seat him in a chair – in contrast to Act II when Stanley resists sitting. Although stage directions tell what Stanley wears, they do not indicate what Goldberg and McCann wear. In Pinter's 1964 production all three were dressed identically. The early editions of the play, and early productions, suggested conformity differently: Stanley wore striped trousers, a black jacket, and a bowler hat.

Written the same year as *The Room* and *The Birthday*

Party, The Dumb Waiter revolves around two people in a room. Whereas *The Birthday Party* chiefly focuses on the victim, *The Dumb Waiter* centres upon victimisers – two hired killers who wait for instructions as to when their victim will enter. While they wait they read a newspaper, they bicker over details, and one of them – to the other's annoyance – frequently asks questions. Strange events occur, such as an envelope sliding under a door. More mysteriously a dumb waiter clatters down with orders for food. While one man is in the toilet the other receives orders from a speaking tube near the dumb waiter. Evidently following them he points his gun at the door to the room, through which his colleague enters, stripped of jacket, tie, and pistol. On this tableau the curtain closes.

The play is about its title, *The Dumb Waiter*, which is ambiguous for it has three possible referents. One is the machine with its unexplained, perhaps inexplicable, descents and ascents. This referent stresses the arbitrary and irrational universe in which man finds himself. Perhaps the title alludes to Gus, the inquisitive killer who, while waiting, foolishly questions his colleague Ben about why people in the newspaper stories did what they did, why it takes the lavatory tank so long to fill, and – more dangerously – matters concerning their job, such as whether Ben ever gets fed up with it and who cleans up after they have killed their victim. Since he questions aspects of the organisation for which he works, he may threaten it. The purpose of a cog is functional. When Gus appears discontent with his function he disturbs the organisation. Perhaps because it is stupid to do this he finds himself, at the end of the play, in a dangerous position. The title may also refer to Ben, the waiter who is dumb in that he displays no intellectual curiosity about motives and actions, and in that he mutely accepts orders.

This dumbness more strongly guarantees survival than the intellectual inquisitiveness of a person who stupidly fails to hold his tongue. Since these possibilities are not mutually exclusive the title may refer to all, playing upon metaphysical, social, and psychological referents.

Among the things that happen on stage – what the audience sees and underlying what it hears – is that the questioner usually receives no answers and that he is placed in a position wherein he might forfeit his life, perhaps because he questions, perhaps arbitrarily. The fervour with which Ben and Gus argue whether the correct phrase is to light the kettle or light the gas suggests that what is at stake is not correct usage. Accompanying stage directions concern facial expression, bodily posture, and nonverbal sound: '*his eyes narrowing*', '*menacing*', '*They stare at each other, breathing hard*', '*grabbing him with two hands by the throat, at arm's length*' (1,141–2). They reveal that the issue is not language but who sets the rules and who obeys.

Despite the rational explanation concerning the erratic toilet – when Gus pulls the chain it does not flush, but later, possibly because of a deficient ballcock, it unexpectedly does – one's chief perception is that arbitrariness and irrationality govern the world of Gus and Ben (and, by extension, ours). When an envelope with matches mysteriously slides under the door the killers can light the stove for tea. Are the unseen forces that control their lives benign? Not necessarily: chance still reigns for the gas goes out and neither has coins for the meter.

By the time the dumb waiter noisily comes down, demanding food, one is accustomed to an arbitrary world in which human beings have insufficient equipment to cope effectively. The disparity between the demands for unusual food and Gus's inadequate supplies are funny, but underlying the comedy one sees a man emptying all he has in order to appease an unseen master and failing to do so, divesting himself of the food that might nourish him (he even says he needs sustenance); and another anxiously urging him to give up all he has and reprimanding him for his inadequacies. In this play the gods may not kill men for sport, but they torment men and might make one kill the other.

The torment, however, is usually comic. In Pinter's earlier plays, such nonrealistic elements as Rose's blindness and Stanley's interrogation are not comic. In *The Dumb Waiter*, demands from above for increasingly unusual dishes (from the conventional braised steak and chips to the unconventional char siu and bean-sprouts) and the incongruity of what the hired killers supply – including crisps and chocolate – are very funny. Also comically incongruous is their shocked and indignant reaction to newspaper stories about the deaths of an old man and a cat, in contrast to their unemotional attitude toward the murder they will commit. In fact incongruity is the basis of much of the play's humour. Gus hopes their victim will not become excited for Gus has a splitting headache. Although he complains that they enter and leave a city at night, he insists they never did a job in Tottenham because he would remember Tottenham. Comedy also derives from repetition, notably the recitation of their instructions when their victim enters, and the subsequent exchange: 'What do we do if it's a girl?' 'We do the same.' 'Exactly the same?' 'Exactly.' 'We don't do anything different?' 'We do exactly the same.' 'Oh' (I,160).

Verbally and nonverbally, early and late scenes connect. 'You kill me', Ben mockingly tells Gus (I,134), whereas at the end of the play it is Ben who may kill him. Late in the play the gunmen repeat their responses to the newspaper stories, but this time they do not read the stories aloud. Death elsewhere, as reported, is comic; but imminent death, in the room, is not comic. Will Gus murder Ben? When they repeat their instructions, Gus's recognition that Ben forgot the injunction for Gus to take out his gun is funny. When at the end Gus appears at the door without his gun, words become actuality and no longer funny. *The Dumb Waiter* is classically symmetrical and creates menace from initially comic elements.

More insulated than a room is a hothouse. As in *The Room*, a character in *The Hothouse* (Roote) repeatedly hits someone until he sinks to the floor. As in *The Birthday Party*, characters drink at a celebration (Christmas). Early in both plays is a story about someone who gave birth. Both contain interrogation scenes with nonrealistic elements. Like Goldberg, Roote employs clichés, such as 'our glorious dead [. . .] who gave their lives so that we might live' and 'by working, by living, by pulling together as one great family, we stand undaunted' (98,144). Like *The Dumb Waiter* it has a story about someone who died. Each play focuses on the staff of an organisation. In each, at least one member of the staff becomes a victim.

The organisation is a government mental institution, one of whose inmates has just given birth. Roote, head of the establishment as it is called, orders Gibbs to find the father – one of the staff, most of whom the mother serviced. Gibbs singles out Lamb whom he interrogates. Although Lamb maintains he is and has always been virgo intacta, Gibbs decides he is the culprit. Before anything can be done, however, the inmates break out and slaughter all the staff but Gibbs, who becomes the new head.

A hothouse is artificially maintained at a high temperature to cultivate plants without normal resistance to cold or adversity. In the staffrooms of the asylum one character reports that the radiator is scalding; another that it is too hot and that the institution has always been overheated. What precipitates the events that lead to the destruction of the staff is real life, which the artificial environment of a hothouse aims to keep out – normal birth, an occurrence that, according to Roote, is unprecedented in this asylum, which is 'so fragile in its conception and execution' that it is sent 'tottering into chaos' (37).

As in Pinter's earlier plays, life is contingent, absurd. Trusting, unsuspecting Lamb learns that membership in an establishment whose values he shares is no proof against destruction. Nor is leadership of that establishment, as Roote discovers. But destruction is not automatic. Absurdly Gibbs survives and flourishes. While he wants to kill the chief and replace him, he does not plan or foresee the cataclysmic events that accidentally result from his action (Lamb, whom he keeps in the interrogation room, is supposed to test the locks of the inmates' cells).

Often menace is comic, as in the interrogation scene which, like that of *The Birthday Party,* contains *non sequiturs* (after questioning Lamb on his sex life, Gibbs asks him to recite the law of the Wolf Cub Pack), two voices speaking with one rhythm ('Do women frighten you?' 'Their clothes?' 'Their shoes?' 'Their voices?' 'Their laughter?' 'Their stares?' 'Their way of walking?' 'Their way of sitting?' 'Their way of smiling?' 'Their way of talking?' (74–5)), and nonrealistic elements (cymbal clashes, a trombone chord, and a bass note substitute for nouns). Menace – no longer funny – erupts as three characters draw knives, but before they use them they hear amplified sounds of a sigh, a keen, and a dying laugh; a blue light glows, and locks, chains, and iron doors sound; dark-gowned patients appear, weaving, slithering about, and whispering.

In contrast to the earlier plays, the menace is explained. Also in contrast, characters articulate the absurdity of their condition, for instance: 'It is absurd. Something's happening. I feel it, I know it, and I can't define it' (122). Symbolism is trite. Apart from the contrived, obvious central metaphor (society as a corrupt mental asylum), Lamb – whom Gibbs calls guilty – wins a dead duck at a raffle.

The play's most effective aspect is its comedy which is often hilarious and is more farcical than in any other play by Pinter. For example, Roote throws a glass of whisky in Lush's face, whereupon Lush calmly refills Roote's glass and both do the same – twice. Comedy also derives from incongruity (a patient died on Thursday but the head of the asylum apparently spoke to him on Friday), the unexpected (demanding to know why he was not informed of a patient's death, Roote is told he signed the death certificate), tautology, and repetition.

Unlike the verbal and scenic links in the earlier (and most of the later) plays, those in *The Hothouse* are conventional. Sometimes passages serve to foreshadow (Lamb's job) or recapitulate (the uprising is attributed to the locktester's not being on duty). At other times sequences provide symmetry: at the end of Act I Lamb sits, silently talking, in the interrogation room (its loudspeakers are off); at the end of Act II he sits there still – but staring as if in a catatonic trance.

Pinter's insistence, in a prefatory note, that he cut but did not change this play, indicates his desire to date it as a product of his youth, not of his more mature period. Yet his 1957 plays are more mature than the 1958 *Hothouse* which, despite several enormously funny scenes, does not repeat their artistry but parodies it. In 1966 Pinter called it 'so heavily satirical' as to be 'quite useless' and its characters 'purely cardboard'. He intentionally tried to make 'an explicit point, that these were nasty people and I disapproved of them. And therefore they didn't begin to live. Whereas in other plays of mine every single character, even a bastard like Goldberg in *The Birthday Party,* I care for'.[8] Unfortunately younger Pinter's critical appraisal of the play seems more valid than that of older Pinter. Fortunately, however, his changed decision about directing his own work seems vindicated, for reports of his production indicate that it was uproariously funny and frequently effective.

The Hothouse dramatises a mental institution; *A Slight Ache*, psychological breakdown. The action of *A Slight Ache* occurs during the summer solstice, the longest day of the year. Flora, whose name is the Roman goddess of flowers and who picks daisies in her daisy apron, cultivates her garden and understands its flowers, which her husband Edward – who remembers 'Especially fauna' (I,183) – does not. Apprehensive about a Matchseller who stands outside the gate, Edward has Flora invite him in. Privately Edward tries to elicit information from him, but the Matchseller says nothing. When Flora is alone with him she is seductive. In Edward's next interview with him, Edward is unable to cope with the Matchseller's silence. Losing control of himself, Edward collapses. Flora puts the Matchseller's tray in her husband's hands and takes the Matchseller into the garden for lunch.

When, at the play's start, a wasp is trapped in a marmalade pot and is about to be killed, Edward feels a slight ache in his eyes. He pours scalding water through the spoonhole, blinding the wasp which he squashes to death. As the wasp peers through the spoonhole at Edward and is vulnerable to the boiling water, Edward (in the next scene) peers through a window in the dark scullery and sees the Matchseller, whose body, he later says, is like jelly and to whom he will become vulnerable. He complains of the brightness outside and Flora observes that his eyes are bloodshot. During his interviews with the Matchseller, his insecurities mount, he recalls blinding sunlight, the ache in his eyes worsens, as does his sight, and he falls to the floor. Edward's physical ache is a manifestation of his psychological ache as he deteriorates to the point of helplessness.

Edward wonders why the Matchseller stands on a lonely country road. As if to announce that such questions are irrelevant, Pinter has Flora state, 'he's not here through any . . . design, or anything' and 'he might just as well stand outside our back gate as anywhere else' (I,189). Pinter focuses on what happens: Edward is insecure (he brags to someone he need not impress), he desperately pleads and is helpless before the Matchseller's remorseless silence, and he deteriorates while his wife, rejecting him, seduces the stranger. She decides to call the Matchseller Barnabas, a name she says Edward would not have guessed. One study of Pinter explains: 'she associates him with sexuality, for Barnabas was an early Christian father who disagreed strongly with St Paul, the apostle of chastity'.[9] Regardless of whether one recognises the allusion, one is aware that Flora thrusts a sexual role on the silent Matchseller, a role that implicitly contrasts him with her husband whom she explicitly refutes by saying that the Matchseller's body is not like jelly.

Verbal comedy derives from repetition ('I say, can you hear me? (*Pause.*) I said, I say, can you hear me?' (I,184)), tautology (asked what the Matchseller is doing, Flora replies that he is selling matches), cross-purposes (Edward's inability to follow his wife's references to honey-suckle and convolvulus), and double entendre (he offers the Matchseller such drinks as Focking Orange and Fuchs-mantel Reisling).

Verbally and otherwise, Pinter connects different sequences. The question of sight relates the title to Edward's eyes. The first line concerns noticing flowers; soon Edward says he must look; in the final part of his last speech he twice uses the verb 'to see' in the past tense when talking of himself but twice uses the verb 'to look' in the present when referring to the Matchseller. Edward claims to be writing an essay on the dimensionality and continuity of space and time – which the play dramatises. He says he was once in the same position the Matchseller is in now and advises him to get a good woman (he later obtains Edward's). When the Matchseller sits in one of Edward's chairs, Pinter links the men in time and space. Edward bought the chair 'When I was a young man. You too, per-haps' (I,187). Soon after Edward tells the Matchseller that everything in the house has been polished, Flora tells him she polished the whole house for him – another dramatic continuum. She feels she saw him when he was younger and raped her; now, she seduces him – still another continuum. When Edward falls down the Matchseller rises – spatial replacement. At the start of the play, Edward and Flora breakfast; at the end, she and the Matchseller go alone to lunch as Flora gives Edward his tray – the dimensions of space replaced in a continuity of time.

In *A Slight Ache* the menace is an external manifestation of internal, psychological disturbance. Confronted with it, the sheltering individual cannot maintain his equilibrium. Moreover the appearance of the Matchseller – who for no logical reason stands by the back gate, worries the man of the house and sexually provokes the woman – is gratuitous. The destruction of the man and the renewal of the woman are contingent, absurd. Similarly the menace that over-comes the comedy need not menace. Edward's and Flora's subjectivity determines their relationship with the visitor.

4
Toward Greater Realism

The title *A Night Out* would seem to herald a departure from the interiors of Pinter's first five plays. With the benefit of hindsight, however, the departure probably derives from the medium for which he wrote the work, radio, which permits an easier flow through different locales than the stage does. When writing a play for the stage, in contrast to writing one for another theatrical medium (as he originally wrote *A Slight Ache* for radio), Pinter usually thinks in terms of a clearly delineated space. The chief exceptions are the lyric *Silence*, whose dramaturgy is unique in the Pinter canon, and the multi-scenic *Betrayal*, whose structure may derive partly from his cinema experience. Furthermore the intrinsic quality of *A Night Out* suggests an emphasis not on the last word of the title but on the first two. Departure is temporary.

Nevertheless this play, like the two that follow, is less enigmatic, mysterious, or unrealistic than Pinter's earlier work. No character suddenly and unexpectedly goes blind. Though interrogation is disturbing, it is not irrational or self-contradictory. No character leaves through one door and returns through another, and unseen forces do not demand exotic food. Neither does a vendor unaccountably stand on a lonely country road, nor does his presence have bizarre effects upon a middle-aged couple.

While the trio of plays discussed in this chapter are to some extent enigmatic, their enigmas differ in kind from those of the earlier works. The nature of what is undefined is more specific and whatever mysterious qualities it may possess, the unreal is not among them. In short, these plays move toward greater realism.

Since his father died, Albert, the young protagonist of *A Night Out,* lives with his mother who henpecks him and treats him like a child. Pestering him about leading a clean life, which means not seeing women, his mother tries in vain to prevent him from attending a retirement party for Ryan who works for the same firm as Albert. At the party, Gidney taunts him and arranges for Eileen to lead him on so that he can observe the shy, repressed young man's embarrassment. During a toast for Ryan, Eileen screams. Someone touched her, she says – indecently, she implies – and she accuses the innocent Albert who has no notion of what he is supposed to have done. As the smile on old Ryan's face reveals, his was the hand that strayed. Nastily Gidney harasses the hapless Albert and calls him a mother's boy. Stung by the truth of the accusation, Albert hits him and leaves. When he returns home his mother badgers him. At his wit's end, he raises a clock above his head to hit her. In the next scene he picks up a prostitute with pretensions of gentility. Each lies to the other about his status and breeding. But her orders to be neat in her room remind him of his mother's. He intimidates her and threatens to kill her with the clock. Next he is at home with his mother, who scolds him for having raised his hand to her. He did not kill her after all, but only made a futile, impotent gesture.

Pinter's usual comic techniques are in evidence: repetition (whether a girl is named Betty or Hetty), tautology (the reason Albert wants a tie, he says, is to put it on), the unexpected (when Eileen claims someone touched her, a character asks, 'Where?' (I,226)), and contradiction ('I'm no different from any other girl. In fact, I'm better' (I,239)). Except for questions of how Albert will behave in different situations with women, little underlies the surface of this realistic play, a psychological study of a harassed mother's boy who leaves his abode but who returns after only a single night out.

In *The Room* and *The Birthday Party* characters who hope they have sanctuary try to defend themselves from intruders; in *A Night Out* a character tries to break out of his soul-stultifying haven. In contrast to all, a character in *The Caretaker* aims to find sanctuary. Unlike *The Room, The Birthday Party*, and *The Hothouse*, no unrealistic elements erupt in *The Caretaker*; yet, as in *The Hothouse*, electro-shock treatment in a mental institution figures prominently in it; and, as in *A Night Out*, its realistic mode is unbroken. Pinter professes not to understand why some people regard *The Caretaker* as strange; he calls it 'a very straightforward and simple play' (II,10).

On the level of plot, it is. Aston has rescued Davies, a frightened, down-at-heel old man, from a fight and brings him to his flat where he offers lodging and money until Davies pulls himself together. Mick, Aston's younger brother, intimidates Davies, then ingratiates himself with him. Separately each brother offers him a job as caretaker. Davies tries to play off one against the other but at the end is rejected by both.

Yet there is more to *The Caretaker* than this bare-bones plot summary suggests. In his conversation with Terence

Rattigan, reported in chapter 1, Pinter makes it clear that in his own mind the title refers to Davies. But Davies does not get the job, and Aston, in effect, is caretaker for Mick who owns the house, while Mick is caretaker of his brother who may be mentally unstable. Like *The Dumb Waiter*, the title *The Caretaker* has an apparently simple meaning yet is really ambiguous.

So is Aston's explanation of his experiences – his only long speech and the longest in the play. If, as he implies, he suffered brain damage as a result of electric-shock treatment, all of his statements are not necessarily accurate. If he did not, they may still be inaccurate since much of what he relates occurred when he was a minor, over ten years before. As in Pinter's other plays, what happens is more important than what happened. The fact that the speech is long, in marked contrast to Aston's uncompleted or clipped speeches before and after, suggests that it is important to him, perhaps that it has taken him time to formulate it or to build up courage to reveal so much. In context, as one critic observes, 'This long speech comes at a time when the relationship with Davies is deteriorating, and it has a function as a response to that deterioration'.[1] Aston is trying to explain his background and condition, possibly in an appeal for understanding and sympathy from the man he befriended. That man not only fails to respond but he later warns Aston he might be recommitted, calls him half crazy, and boasts that he himself has 'never been inside a nut-house!' (II,76).

Just as Aston fails to elicit sympathy, so Davies, earlier, fails to elicit confirmation of his dignity. Describing the fight from which Aston rescued him, he says, 'When he come at me tonight I told him. Didn't I? You heard me tell him, didn't you?' Because Aston's noncorroboration suggests a negative answer – 'I saw him have a go at you'

(II,17–18) – it deprives Davies of dignity.

Also underlying the words of Davies and Aston – the subtext – are efforts to establish friendship but hesitancy to reveal themselves (the truth will make you weak, each fears, therefore more vulnerable). Thus when Davies asks how many rooms Aston has, Aston (who does not own the house) evasively says they are out of commission and when Aston asks whether Davies is Welsh, Davies evasively says he has been around. While each man wants friendship, his refusal to communicate in terms the other proposes prevents him from getting it. 'Well, I reckon', says Davies, without finishing his sentence; and Aston says, 'Well, I mean', without completing his (II,51). As important as their failure to articulate, during those occasions when they do not avoid articulating, is their effort to do so.

In contrast to their disjointed and inarticulate speech is Mick's loquacity and articulateness, but he too produces incomprehension, which is partly his intent. Why Mick terrorises Davies by forcing him to the floor and interrogating him is not immediately clear. What is clear, and theatrically powerful, is that he does this. Threat is the mood, the establishment of power the meaning. In their first encounter Mick barely permits Davies to speak, and his proliferation of words confuses his victim and nullifies him, destroying his identity and even his sex. According to Mick, Davies reminds him of his uncle's brother (he does not say father or uncle) but he is unsure whether the uncle was the brother or the reverse, and he never called the man uncle. That man, he tells the decrepit Davies, had 'Very much your build. Bit of an athlete'. He was Davies's 'spitting image' and married not a Chinese woman but 'a Chinaman' (II,40). Mick's next pronouncements further reduce Davies's stature. He resembles someone Mick knew in Shoreditch but who lived in Aldgate, played cricket in Finsbury Park, was raised in

Putney, and so forth, with such a profusion of place names and bus numbers as to wear Davies down. Further establishing Mick's power are his changing tones of voice – within half a page – from '*A shout*' to '*amiable*' (II,42). However, the atmosphere of terror and helplessness has none of the unrealistic qualities of the interrogation in *The Birthday Party* or *The Hothouse*.

The quality and context of language, not its denotations or connotations, establish meaning. Mick's decorative ideas, which he implies Davies might execute – teal-blue linoleum squares, charcoal-grey worktops, off-white pile linen rug, afromosia teak veneer, and the like – convey not a coherent interior design but a coherent mockery of Davies. This, not the decorative scheme, is the scene's subject.

Despite its realistic detail *The Caretaker* undercuts veracity. Real is not necessarily true. At times contradictions occur in two successive sentences, as when Aston says, 'I used to have kind of hallucinations. They weren't hallucinations' (II,63–4). Little is what it appears to be. Davies goes by another name. One brother lives in the house but another owns it and lives elsewhere. Such undercutting creates meaning, an ambience of insecurity and, in its wake, fear and danger.

Action, not words, often conveys a scene's dramatic point. When Mick snatches the bag Aston gives Davies, and eludes him, refusing to surrender it, his humiliation of the defenceless old man is clearly a theme. Also noteworthy, Aston sides with Davies against his brother. Verbally Aston has been unable to express friendship, but by picking up the bag and giving it to Davies he establishes a bond, which he confirms not by articulating it but by conversing with Davies on a different subject, thereby ignoring his brother, who leaves. At the heart of the scene, clear in performance, is not the subject of conversation but the side-taking and, in consequence, the physical dislocation of the person whose side is not taken.

The business of grabbing, giving, and taking Davies's bag is farcically funny and becomes funnier when Aston, having taken it from Mick, pauses and returns it to Mick who, accustomed to giving it to someone other than the person from whom he gets it, mechanically gives it to Davies. Comedy derives from character, as when Davies, trying to ingratiate himself with Aston, agrees that a jig saw is useful, then asks what a jig saw is. The play also contains Pinter's customary verbal comedy of repetition ('I'll have to tar it over.' 'You're going to tar it over?' 'Yes.' 'What?' 'The cracks.' 'You'll be tarring over the cracks on the roof?' (II,46)), tautology (the explanation as to who lives next door is 'neighbours' (II,21)), incongruity (Mick invites the old tramp to listen to Tchaikovsky with him), and *non sequitur* (after threatening Davies in the darkness with a vacuum cleaner, Mick unplugs it, inserts a light bulb, and calmly explains that he has been spring cleaning).

Verbally Pinter connects scenes. 'You're stinking the place out', Mick tells Davies (II,44). Later, when Davies calls Aston's shed stinking, he refers not to odour but to offensiveness. Vehemently Aston twice denies that it stinks and uses his brother's phrase, 'You've been stinking the place out' (II,78). Offended, Davies repeats the word as a threat. He relates the exchange to Mick, who first reassures him that he does not stink and that if he did Mick would be the first to tell him – as, indeed, he was. Shortly thereafter he tells Davies, 'you stink from arse-hole to breakfast time' (II,83).

'As far as I'm concerned', Pinter has said, '*The Caretaker* is funny, up to a point. Beyond that point it ceases to be funny, and it was because of that point that I wrote it.'[2]

Actually the play is more complex. Each of its first two acts, and the first four dialogues of the third, employ this dramatic movement, from comedy to the cessation of comedy, a movement that increases in tempo in the last act. This movement enforces Pinter's theme, for when laughter stops, the turn from comic to noncomic signals a turn, for Davies, from security to insecurity. When Mick physically threatens him at the end of Act I, laughter stops. In Act II menace gives an edge to laughter, but it is present until Aston begins his recollection at the end of the act. In the first four dialogues of Act III laughter stops when Davies is rejected or when he leaves; in the fifth dialogue laughter is gone, for his rejection is total. In the first, Mick warmly and vividly tells Davies his plans to decorate the flat, but he abruptly concludes with the statement that its residents would be his brother and himself. When the old man asks, 'What about me?' (II,70), comedy stops. Mick does not reply, leaving Davies to plead with him, and he departs when he hears Aston enter below. Next, Davies is comically crotchety about the shoes and laces Aston brings him, but Aston, noncomically, leaves during his grumbling. In the third dialogue the old man whines and complains, but when he taunts his benefactor for having been in a lunatic asylum and flashes a knife at him, laughter stops and Aston demands he leave. The fourth follows a similar pattern. Mick mocks Davies's pretensions, reviles him, and with a sudden burst of violence smashes the Buddha statue, ending comedy. In the scene's final line, Davies echoes his earlier question, 'What about me?' (II,83). As before, Mick does not reply, a silent rejection. In the last dialogue, which is not funny, Davies pleads with Aston to be reinstated. Aston either responds negatively or implies as much by silence.

Part of Pinter's patterning is his balancing of subjects. In the first act laughter results from Davies's attempts to ingratiate himself with Aston; in the last scene no laughter results from these efforts. The play's first words are friendly: Aston invites Davies to sit and offers to help him; at the end he tells Davies to leave and ignores his pleas.

To convey what happens, Pinter employs visual as well as verbal means. In fact, visual devices connect the ends of the three acts. The close of Act I expresses menace in terms of physical action: Mick seizes Davies's arm and twists it up his back, forces him to the floor, presses him down when he starts to rise, and throws his trousers at him. At the end of Act II the audience hears Aston's long speech, but it sees the gradual exclusion of Davies: during the speech the room darkens; by its end, only Aston is clearly visible; like the objects in the room, Davies is in shadow. At the close of the last act the audience hears Davies's pleas while it sees Aston, unmoving, face the window, his back to the old man. In visual terms Davies is threatened, extinguished, and rejected.

Pinter also uses the visual to balance and somewhat leaven the rejection that concludes the play. In Act II, after the visual comedy of the bag-taking, Aston sides with the stranger against his brother. At the end of the play, after he has told Davies to leave and before he conclusively turns his back on him, the brothers face each other. '*They look at each other. Both are smiling, faintly*' (III,84). The adverb ensures against making too much of the pantomime, but the smiles, however faint, suggest reconciliation. The intrusive stranger may be expelled, but the sibling bond is, if only somewhat, restored.

Part of the visual qualities of the play derive from its setting, which includes a vast quantity of junk. Some of the properties are traditional symbols (an electric plug Aston tries to fix and a gas stove Davies fears might be connected) but, more important, these properties form a visual, atmospheric envelope for the play. The scenic clutter and disarray reflect the mind of the room's occupant, the absence of an orderly world in which everything has a place, and only makeshift means to cope with difficulties (a bucket to catch rain from a leaking roof). Realistic, the setting matches the play's dialogue and action. Like them, it suggests more than the literal.

Unlike the realism of *The Caretaker*, that of *Night School* suggests little more than the literal. Walter, a petty forger, returns to his aunts' home after a stay in jail, to discover that they have let his room to Sally who claims to be a school teacher and to spend three evenings a week at night school where she studies foreign languages. From her room, Walter steals a photograph that suggests she is a night-club hostess. He shows it to Solto, a higher level criminal than Walter, and asks him to locate the club. Solto does, is attracted to Sally, proposes they have a weekend together, and reveals the matter of the photograph. He tells Walter he was unable to find the club. Without confronting either the aunts or Walter, Sally vacates the premises, leaving a note and a photograph of herself with children in a school playground.

With the possible exception of *The Hothouse, Night School* may be as close to a formula play as Pinter has written. Although it contains his trademarks, including a desire for a room as haven, they appear to be grafted onto an essentially conventional drama that simply asks and (unusual for Pinter) simply answers such questions as whether Sally really goes to night school, whether Walter will retrieve his room, whether Solto will find the club, and whether Sally will discover what Walter has done.

Although the title obviously refers to the lie Sally tells Walter and his aunts, the lie becomes true in one sense: at the club she learns of Walter's action. The title suggests a tissue of lies (Solto's cry of poverty, Walter's boast that he is an armed robber), but the tissue is thinner than usual for Pinter.

What happens stays very much on the surface and supposed enigmas are not enigmatic. An early statement that Sally perfumes herself heavily is a conventional clue that her story about night school is untrue. Because Solto confirms Walter's interpretation of Sally's photograph, Walter's stratagems in his second encounter with her are obvious. By persuading her to drink more than a nice young lady is expected to drink, by provoking calm responses to tales of criminal life, by leading her to flirt with him as he flirts with her, and by ordering her to cross and uncross her legs, stand and rise, as one might order a prostitute (and as Albert similarly orders one in *A Night Out*), Walter makes her confirm his suspicion.

Since Pinter is a deft writer of comic dialogue, his success is chiefly on this level. One finds his customary comedy based on repetition (an aunt has not been well but 'Middling. Only middling.' 'I'm only middling as well.' 'Yes, Annie's only been middling.' (II,201)), incongruity (the petty criminal is indignant that a school teacher occupies his room), contradiction (Solto is almost one of the family, but he has not come to tea for months), misunderstanding ('a six-foot-ten Lascar from Madagascar.' 'From Madagascar?' 'Sure. A Lascar.' 'Alaska?' 'Madagascar' (II,212)), and tautology (asked what she and Solto were doing on the dance floor, Sally replies, 'Dancing!' (II,229)).

Initially Pinter shared this view of *Night School*. As Esslin reports, he was dissatisfied with it, did not publish it, and refused to permit further performances; 'he once said that he repudiated the play because it struck him as too obviously and mechanically "Pinteresque", as though it were a copy of a play by Pinter rather than a genuine work.'[3] Since he later revised it and sanctioned publication and performance, he no longer holds this view. Regardless of the validity of his or my judgement (that the play, though clever, is lesser Pinter), *Night School* supplies additional confirmation to what *A Night Out* and *The Caretaker* suggest, a dramatic development from unrealistic elements toward greater realism.

5
Struggles for Power

Although struggles for power form the basis of conflict in earlier plays by Pinter, they are especially prominent in the plays analysed in this chapter. In them potential victims fight victimisation, even try to victimise their antagonists; and who is victor, who victim, is often ambiguous. *Night School* adumbrates this question. Although Walter succeeds in regaining his room, he loses Sally; although she is dispossessed, she does not fall under his control.

In their battles Pinter's characters use words and silences as weapons. As Quigley says, 'no matter how one is addressed there is an implicit demand for a particular range of response. To respond within that range is to accept the relationship on the terms of the first speaker; to reply outside of that range is to qualify or reject the common ground of the relationship as envisaged by the first speaker. Clearly, the response of silence is frequently of the latter kind.'[1] In *The Caretaker,* when Davies asks Aston to confirm that he reprimanded the man who went for him earlier, Aston replies outside the range, saying only that he saw the

man have a go at him; and the second time Davies asks
Mick what will happen to him, Mick's silence is a rejection
of him.

'Somebody's taking the Michael', Stanley tells Meg in
The Birthday Party (1,31). His phrase is a variant of the
cockney expression 'taking the mickey' or 'taking the piss',
which Roote in *The Hothouse* employs verbatim ('Are you
taking the piss out of me?' (18)) and euphemistically
('you're not by any chance taking the old wee-wee out of
me, are you?' (27)). However modified, the phrase means
to taunt or mock someone, lightly or cruelly, thereby getting the better of him. According to Peter Hall, veiled
mockery is 'at the base of a good deal of [Pinter's] work'
and gives meaning to textual ambiguities. Part of such
mockery 'is that you should not be quite sure whether the
piss is being taken or not. In fact, if you know I'm taking the
piss, I'm not really doing it very well.'[2] Whatever their real
passions, characters try to present a facade of coolness and
detachment. Although the play's surface may seem to lack
conflict, the subtext, perceptible in performance, contains
fury. As Hall states, 'to show emotion in Pinter's world is
[. . .] a weakness, which is mercilessly punished by the other
characters. You have to construct the mask of the character
– because all Pinter's characters have masks [. . .] But the
mask almost never slips.'[3] When it does, the result can be
catastrophic.

Verbal or silent thrusts and parries, and piss-taking or
donning masks, are not mutually exclusive. Piss-taking may
employ or underlie verbal or silent tactics. Masks may conceal them. In their struggles for power, Pinter's characters
use some or all of these methods.

While *The Dwarfs* is apparently plotless, character relationships change between beginning and end. At the start,
Len, Pete, and Mark are friends, though their friendship

contains elements of mutual distrust and jealousy. At the end, friendship between Pete and Mark dissolves, and Len seems to be isolated from both.

The dwarfs may be Len's *alter ego*. He has summoned them, he says, to observe Pete and Mark closely. 'They don't stop work until the job in hand is finished, one way or another. [. . .] We're all going to keep a very close eye on you two. Me and the dwarfs' (II,102). When his friends appear to have left Len for good, the primary job of the dwarfs is over and they leave. Dwarfs may be much smaller than usual in size or (like Len) in stature; they may (like Len) have small or negligible endowments; and they may be short, misshapen, and ugly creatures who (like Len) are duplicitous and insincere. Treacherously Len destroys the friendship of Pete and Mark.

When Len and Pete, with apparent calm, comment on Mark's flat, the dramatic subject is less the flat than the struggle as to who will impose his view on the other. Without seeming to do so, they take the piss out of each other. As if in friendly jest, Len denigrates Mark: 'You'd think a man like him would have a maid, wouldn't you, to look after the place while he's away, to look after his milk? Or a gentleman. A gentleman's gentleman. Are you quite sure he hasn't got a gentleman's gentleman tucked away somewhere, to look after the place for him?' Lightly Pete uses Len's term as a jeer: 'You're the only gentleman's gentleman he's got.' Len pauses – perhaps thrown off balance, a result of Pete's success – and attempts amiably to keep his mask by turning Pete's specific identification into a conditional abstraction: 'Well, if I'm his gentleman's gentleman, I should have been looking after the place for him' (II,92–3).

Jockeyings for position, often in a superficially light manner, help create the play's ambience and suggest its subjects: distrust in the guise of trust, insecurity underlying friendship, and the desire to control others. *The Dwarfs* begins with Pete's refusal to respond to Len's effort to interest him in a recorder's malfunction. At first, Pete greets Len's question with silence, thereby refusing to acknowledge Len's ability to command the terms of the conversation. Then he successfully dictates a different subject, tea. Len's compulsive chatter – mocking Mark's food supply, implying that Mark over-eats, insisting that while others may change he does not, and outlining his regular eating habits – reveals an inability to control the conversation and (by excessive explanation) the insecurity that underlies a stable routine. Only when he begins to repeat, for the fifth time, that he runs downstairs and upstairs while preparing food and working, does Pete acknowledge that he has listened, and the acknowledgement takes the form of an appeal to stop talking. Subsequently Pete answers none of Len's questions about his shoes. Whereas Len is insecure, Peter controls the situation.

In *The Dwarfs* comedy derives from piss-taking, as in Len's mockery of the profession of people in whose company he thinks Mark has been – actors. 'Does it please you when you walk onto a stage and everybody looks up and watches you? Maybe they don't want to watch you at all. Maybe they'd prefer to watch someone else' (II,98). As this example indicates, repetition is part of the mockery. It is also part of the conflict when Len tries to dictate the subject of conversation to Mark, who cannily and comically evades it:

Do you believe in God?
What?
Do you believe in God
Who?

61

God.
God?
Do you believe in God?
Do I believe in God?
Yes.
Would you say that again? (II,111).

Verbally and visually Pinter links Len's fear of change and desire for stability with his successful effort to change Mark's and Pete's friendship and thereby create a more central, therefore more stable, position for himself. To Len the stability of his possessions is undermined by what he perceives to be a moving room. Soon, in what may be an attempt to frighten Mark, he talks about rooms that change shape at will. When, still later, he describes the fluidity of human identity and the imperfection and constant change of another person's perception of oneself, he shifts the subject to Pete who he says considers Mark a fool. Mark responds not to instability and imperfect perception but to the statement about Pete who later confirms it. Yet Len's success in destroying their friendship does not necessarily create stability for himself. The opening stage directions designate the specific locales of different stage areas and also an '*area of isolation*' (II,91). In it the solitary Len observes Pete, then Mark. After Len severs the bond between Pete and Mark, he stands in the isolation area. Before their confrontation, they visit him in the hospital. Friendly they sit on his bed, but he rudely reprimands them for an infraction of hospital rules and orders them to sit on chairs. Instead they leave. When Pete calls Mark a fool, Len is not present. The text gives no indication that Len knows what happened, which parallels what had happened at the hospital: departure after an insult. In the final scene Len is alone in the isolation area. While his speech apparently refers to the dwarfs, it is also suggestive of his relationship to the two men. He considers himself left in the lurch and observes the change about him. In contrast to previous occasions, everything is bare, but it is also clean, even scrubbed, and he sees a shrub and a flower. Although foliage may suggest a change for the better, the cleanliness may suggest isolation. His situation is ambiguous. Victorious in his effort to destroy a friendship, he may be a victim of his success.

Ambiguities pervade *The Collection* in which James confronts Bill with his wife Stella's assertion that she and Bill cuckolded him during a dress designers' collection at Leeds. Bill, a young homosexual living with Harry, who is older, denies the accusation. Other, conflicting stories emerge: Bill accompanied Stella to her room but did nothing; they kissed but did no more; they sat in the lounge and discussed but did not commit adultery; they did not meet. Seeking the truth, and perhaps fascinated by the man his wife (or he) would find attractive, James visits Bill again. Aiming to preserve his relationship with Bill from outside interference, Harry visits Stella who denies everything. Harry confronts the other men with that denial, but Bill fails to confirm this story and Stella fails to confirm anything to James.

On a literal level the title refers to the dress collection at Leeds, the setting of the alleged adultery. *The Collection* also describes the dramatic form of the play. At a clothing collection designers present a new line of fashions, or goods, to prospective buyers. In the play the new fashion in the Hornes's marriage is adultery, presented by Stella, a designer, to James, who in a manner of speaking 'buys the goods'. But a collection has more than one item. In addition to adultery are the various possibilities mentioned in the last paragraph. Often a designer's collection mixes and matches different items of apparel. In this designing playwright's presentation are dramatic patterns, parallels, and variations suggestive of a mix-and-match combination of clothes in an elegant fashion show. Mirrors provide parallel images. At one point Bill calls them deceptive, but James, after looking at his and Bill's reflections, thinks not. As evidence that an ordinary mirror gives an accurate reflection, one can do what James does: look at someone, then at his reflection. Yet in so far as mirrors show the reverse of what one places before it, they deceive. As evidence, hold this page before a mirror and try to read its reflection. In *The Collection* scenes mirror but do not exactly reflect. Early James reports that his wife scratched Bill, whereupon Bill shows his unscratched hand. Later Bill raises his hand to protect his face from a knife James throws at him and catches the blade, which cuts his hand. As James points out, Bill has a scar after all. In this parallel scene the mirror might deceive, but so might Bill's statement in the earlier scene.

The dramatis personae form a mix-and-match combination: two couples, two men possibly cuckolded. But the pairs do not precisely mirror each other, for one is heterosexual, the other homosexual. Still they may do so in different mixtures, for Bill may like James have had a heterosexual relationship with Stella, and an incipient homosexual relationship between James and Bill may parallel the one between Bill and Harry. Mirrors may reflect *and* deceive.

Mixing and matching the four characters, the play is mainly a series of dialogues *à deux*, like a well co-ordinated outfit. The only couple not to engage in such dialogue are Bill and Stella, the only characters who know what happened at Leeds. If Pinter were to present them together, they might tell the truth, but he could also reveal the truth by having one confirm the other's story. His refusal to do either suggests not that he cannot (the truth is hidden, not unverifiable) but that the dramatic focus is elsewhere. (Apropos, the persistent question of what happened between Bill and Stella skilfully masks a dramatic convenience: how Harry obtains the telephone number and address of the Hornes, whose name he does not know.)

Dramatically what happens, which is more important than what happened, is a series of struggles for power. For example, when James visits Bill, who has just gone, he meets Harry and asks, 'When will he be in?' 'I can't say. Does he know you?' 'I'll try some other time then.' 'Well, perhaps you'd like to leave your name. I can tell him when I see him.' 'No, that's all right. Just tell him I called.' 'Tell him who called?' 'Sorry to bother you' (II,126–7). In their thrusts and parries each tries to dictate the terms of the conversation, to obtain information, and to avoid revealing information. The result is stalemate. Harry does not say he does not know when Bill will return, but that he cannot say; and James does not answer Harry's questions. Every scene contains a power struggle. James tries to make Harry awaken Bill, but Harry refuses; Stella attempts to get James to tell her his exact plans for the day, but he is evasive; James aims to force Bill to confirm his wife's account of what happened between them, but Bill makes the event more problematic; and so forth. In the final scene Stella gains or regains power over James, and her knowledge of what happened between her and Bill enables her to control the situation, just as Bill's knowledge enabled him to control the situation in an earlier, parallel scene.

Observing these conflicts, the audience occupies the same position as the character who lacks knowledge and directly experiences his dilemma. When Bill begins a short speech, 'I was nowhere near Leeds last week', and ends it,

'I . . . just don't do such things' (II,131), knowledge that the first statement is false casts doubt upon the
second, which one would ordinarily credit. A string of such
ambiguities helps create an aura of mystery.

At times, mystery leads to menace, but there is no clear-
cut distinction between victim and victimiser. With a sudden move forward, James startles Bill into falling over a
pouffe (a visual pun) onto the floor. Standing over him
menacingly, James makes him relate what happened at
Leeds, but when James disbelieves Bill's denial of adultery
and repeats his wife's assertion that they were sitting on the
bed, Bill – following a silence, thus deliberately – says, 'Not
sitting. Lying' (II,137). After James employs physical
violence on Bill, throwing a knife at him, Harry employs
verbal violence. Talking to James about Bill, as if he were
not present, Harry uses language to take the piss out of Bill
and assert his own power. 'Bill's a slum boy', Harry says
suavely, with 'a slum sense of humour' and 'a slum mind';
he repeats 'slum' several times, identifying it with the rot-
ten and putrid, and he further demeans his lover by calling
him 'boy' (II,154–5). Wounded by Harry's verbal assault as
he had been by James's physical attack, Bill revenges himself with words. He gives a different story from both of
Stella's – thereby casting doubt on her reassurance and on
his earlier denial of adultery.

As in *The Collection,* sex is the point of departure of *The
Lover* where it is more prominent. At its start Richard is
complaisant about his wife Sarah's taking a lover during the
afternoon while he is at the office. Later he admits he has a
whore. When he leaves, Sarah changes from a demure to a
tight, low-cut, black dress and from low-heeled to high-
heeled shoes. She admits her lover, Max, who turns out to
be Richard, dressed not in a business suit but tieless in a
suede jacket. They enact seduction games. Although he

wants to terminate their roles of lover and whore, she seduces him into continuing. At the end, however, these roles are no longer separable from their roles as husband and wife.

The most notable characteristic of the title is that it is singular. It refers neither to the couple nor to Richard, a husband who works at an office in the City – when he does work, for he is evidently so well off that he need not remain there for several consecutive afternoons. It refers to Max who, though Richard's *alter ego*, has a different identity: lover. Consistent with the play's conclusion, the title also suggests the triumph of role, and relationship with the woman, of lover over husband.

This triumph is what develops during the play. At first husband and wife discuss her lover. Then they change into lover and whore. As both lover and husband the man tries to stabilise their relationship as conventionally marital, but the woman stabilises it as sexually nonmarital. *The Lover* contrasts asexual marriage with highly sexual non-marriage. The triumph of the latter is the triumph of sex over convention and the woman's desire over the man's. The play's ambience reflects this bifurcation. As husband and wife, Richard and Sarah engage in light, sophisticated banter. As lover and whore, they engage in seduction and the ambience is sexual.

Underlying both badinage and sexuality is a struggle for domination. To control the conversation is to dominate. Richard wishes to talk of himself at the office, Sarah to discuss his relationship with his mistress; he tries to change the subject to the sunset, but she succeeds in making him discuss his sex life. As if in revenge, he changes the terms of her subject. He has no mistress, he claims, only a whore, who is not worth discussing since she is comparable to a quick cup of cocoa while the oil and water in his car are checked. Richard's denigrating description of his whore as a functionary whose job is solely to please actually demeans his wife, who knows he speaks of her, and his disparaging remarks about her lover threaten that relationship between them, as Sarah also recognises, for she next seeks and gets confirmation that Richard is happy, not jealous. In her view, 'things are beautifully balanced' (II,173). At issue is whether they will remain balanced.

Partly comedy derives from Pinter's familiar devices, including repetition ('Bad traffic?' 'No. Quite good traffic, actually.' 'Oh, good' (II,162)), clichés (after discussing their extramarital relationships, Richard remarks that frankness is essential to a healthy marriage), and incongruity (Richard demands his wife terminate her relationship with her lover in terms appropriate to business: 'Perhaps you would give him my compliments, by letter if you like, and ask him to cease his visits from (*He consults calendar.*) – the twelfth inst' (II,190)). Comedy also derives from unexpected inversions of conventional attitudes (at the start of the play Richard casually inquires whether his wife's lover will visit her that day, then wishes her a pleasant afternoon).

Verbally Pinter connects the different relationships and by so doing he places them in jeopardy. Max applies the same attributes to his whore (grace, elegance, and wit) that Richard applies to his wife but that (as Richard) he says do not pertain to a whore. Later he confuses her by contradicting himself. Max calls her too bony and insufficiently plump for his taste; Richard tells her he likes his whore because she is getting thinner, then that he paid her off because she was too bony.

Richard's derogatory remarks about his whore and his wife's lover foreshadow his explicit wish to end that relationship, which Sarah does not foresee. She is surprised and disturbed when Max declares it must stop, and she fails to seduce him. When Richard too demands it must end, she is distraught. This time, however, she succeeds in seducing him. But she does so as a whore, manipulating husband into the role of lover and making him regard her as a whore, which in the play's final line he calls her. Although she says, in the seduction game she persuades him to play, that she is trapped by him, it is Richard who is trapped by her. His role of lover invades and dominates his marital world. Things are no longer beautifully balanced, as Sarah claims earlier. The enactment, sexual seduction, is the subject.

Like *The Dwarfs*, *The Basement* is concerned with friendship and shifting allegiances. Like *The Collection* and *The Lover*, its basis is a sex triangle. Unlike *The Lover*, the two men are different personae. The figures in *The Basement* – Stott, Law, and Jane – are the virile man, the inept man, and the girl. At the start Law invites Stott to stay in his home. Stott brings Jane with him. Gradually she transfers her allegiance to Law. The end of the play returns to its beginning, with Stott inviting Law into what is now his home.

The title refers to Law's basement flat, where most of the action takes place. Unlike *The Attic*, which might hint at mental activity, *The Basement* hints at sex and barely suppressed urges. *The Basement* is also about the flat itself.

The play's meaning inheres in what happens on stage. When Stott enters, Law gives him his possessions (towels and slippers) and invites him to stay as long as he likes. The first scene concludes as Stott and Jane, ignoring Law, remove their clothes, get into Law's bed, and make love while Law reads a Persian love manual. Early on Law tries to dominate Jane by demonstrating how much better he knows Stott than she does, but because her suggestively negative responses are *pro forma* – chiefly 'No' and 'Never'

(III,157–8) – they are an implicit refusal to converse in his terms, a rejection bolstered by her physical activity while he talks: building a sandcastle, which in performance occupies her attention more than his words. When Law tries to persuade Stott that the basement flat is too small for three people, Stott's response – a string of negative phrases, 'No, no. Not at all' (III,163–4) – becomes a refusal to comply in Law's terms. Buttressing Stott's assertion of power is physical action: as they talk, Stott walks, stops to pat Law's shoulder, and continues to walk.

Much of the play is very funny. Pinter employs his customary device of repetition:

> Oh, by the way, I've got a friend outside. Can she come in?
> A friend?
> Outside.
> A friend? Outside?
> Can she come in?
> Come in? (III,154–5).

Adding to the humour is the fact that Stott, after two pages of dialogue, casually alludes to someone standing in the rain. Comedy also derives from incongruity, as when Law offers Stott and Jane cocoa and hot chocolate while they undress. Farcically Law – in a search for a Debussy record Stott requests – flings disc after disc against the wall while Jane sits on Stott's lap.

The most striking characteristic of *The Basement*, visually connecting its scenes while conveying their essence, is the changing set decorations. Pinter wrote the play at approximately the same time that he wrote the movie *The Servant*, in which set decorations show whether the servant or the fiancée is the more powerful influence on the master. To be

1a. *The Homecoming,* London 1965: Teddy (Michael Bryant), Ruth (Vivien Merchant) Joey (Terence Rigby), Max (Paul Rogers)

1b. *The Homecoming,* London, 1978: Joey (Michael Kitchen), Max (Timothy West)

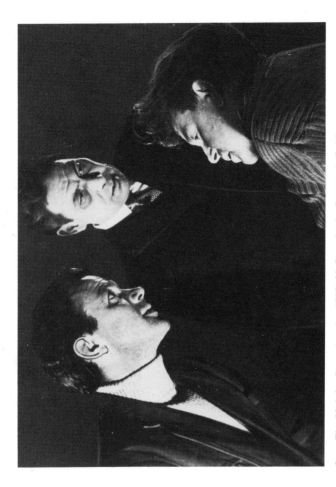

2. *The Birthday Party*, London 1958: McCann (John Stratton), Goldberg (John Slater), Stanley (Richard Pearson)

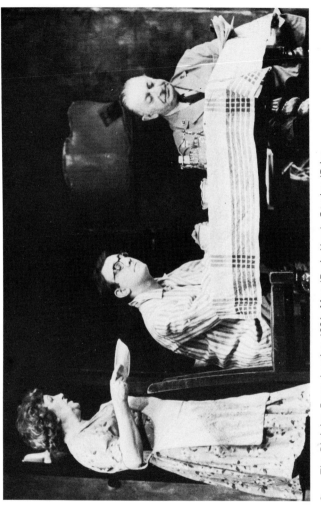

3. *The Birthday Party*, London 1964: Meg (Doris Hare), Stanley (Brian Pringle), Petey (Newton Blick)

4. *The Birthday Party*, New York, 1967: Stanley (James Patterson), Meg (Ruth White), Petey (Henderson Forsythe)

5.   *Old Times*, London 1971: Kate (Dorothy Tutin), Deeley (Colin Blakeley), Anna (Vivien Merchant)

6a. *Betrayal,* London, 1978: Emma (Penelope Wilton), Robert (Daniel Massey) Jerry (Michael Gambon)
6b. *Betrayal,* New York, 1980: Emma (Blythe Danner), Robert (Roy Scheider), Jerry (Raul Julia)

7. *No Man's Land,* London 1975: Spooner (John Gielgud), Hirst (Ralph Richardson)

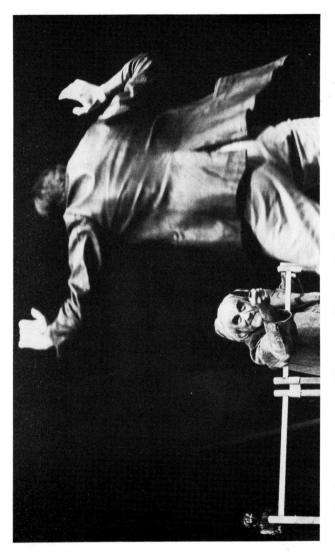

8. *The Caretaker*, London, 1980: Davies (Warren Mitchell), Aston (Jonathan Pryce)

sure Pinter employed this device in his 1955 short story 'The
Examination', where the narrator mentions 'the especial
properties of my abode, bearing the seal and arrangement
of their tenant' (I,254), yet he makes *theatrical* use of shifting scenic accessories for the first time in *The Servant* and
The Basement. Furthermore in this play the setting's visual
manifestation of power precedes its revelation in dialogue.

The first view of the flat shows Law's furnishings, including side tables, plants, armchairs, velvet cloths, and –
notably – book cabinets and bookshelves. Visually Stott
dominates Law when he persuades Law to let him remove
Law's pictures from the wall. In a few moments he verbally
dominates Law by contradicting Law's faintly denigrating
comments on Jane and by implying that his friend knows as
little about him as he does about her. Soon the setting
becomes *'unrecognizable. The furnishing has changed.'*
Bookless it contains a hi-fi cabinet, Scandinavian tables,
and bowls of Swedish glass. The chairs are tubular, the rug
Indian, the floors parquet. The room no longer reflects
Law. As before, and after, the verbal follows the visual:
after permitting Law to assume the role of masterful host at
a bar and to repeat 'same again' five times, Stott calmly
undercuts Law with 'I'll change to Campari', does not deny
Law's compliment that he was unbeatable at squash, and
contradicts Law's statement that Law's style is still deceptive (III,161–2). Indicative that Law resumes a position of
power, the room becomes furnished as it was at the beginning. Next Jane proposes that Law send Stott away so that
they can be alone. Again the room becomes unrecognis-
able. On the walls are tapestries, a Florentine mirror, and
an Italian master. There are marble tiles and marble pillars,
hanging plants and carved golden chairs – but no books. In
command of the flat, Stott verbally commands the start of a
game. He bowls large marbles at Law, who bats them with a

flute. As competition intensifies, Stott bowls marbles that hit Law's knee and forehead, making him fall. With their struggle in the open, the setting becomes completely bare. As they battle with broken milk bottles, the scene ends, failing to demonstrate who is victor. A record plays Debussy – a nonverbal hint that Stott has won the flat. Outside stand Jane and Law. Inside, the room is furnished as it was at the beginning, but it is Stott who reads a book. Although he has the flat, the furnishings seem to cry out for Law, who as if in answer rings the doorbell and is admitted. He and Stott repeat the opening dialogue, but with their roles and speeches reversed. This final scene suggests the start of the cycle already dramatised.

Revolving around senses (eyesight and hearing) and sensuality, *Tea Party* dramatises the deterioration of the head of a firm and the ascension of his wife, brother-in-law, and secretary. The same day Disson acquires a new secretary, Wendy, he meets his brother-in-law to be, Willy; the following day he marries Diana. At the wedding reception Willy eulogises both bride and groom, for Disson's best man, suddenly stricken with the flu, cannot attend. Afterwards Disson invites Willy to join the firm, where he rises to partner. Disson's twin sons by a former marriage take to their stepmother and her brother. Disson's physical powers worsen until he can no longer see (apparently), hear, or move.

The title refers to the climactic scene, the celebration of the first anniversary of Disson's marriage. As in *The Birthday Party*, which also has a titular celebration, the protagonist becomes helpless. Whereas external forces impose upon, terrify, and destroy Stanley, insecurities impose upon and terrify Disson. At the tea party a character asks why Disson did not have a cocktail party. Perhaps Pinter does not want to suggest that Disson's downfall results from excessive alcohol (in an earlier scene, it contributes to his abusiveness). Certainly Disson's blindness and immobility, shocking in themselves, are more shocking in the context of a sedate tea party.

The audience's perception of what happens often lies not in the meaning of words but in their emotional effect. When Willy, at the wedding reception, shifts his eulogy of Disson to praise of Diana, he thereby nullifies the groom and elevates the bride's status. During Disson's honeymoon his persistent questioning as to whether his bride is happier than she has been with any other man reveals his insecurities, as do his assertions that he is not weak, for he protests too much. Despite Disson's aggressiveness he starts to crumble when Diana states that she loved and admired him – the past tense subtly undermining verbs of affection. As evidence of his further loss of power, he follows Willy's warning to watch himself with an offer that Willy become his partner in the firm. Furthermore, as his eyesight begins to deteriorate and he argues with Willy, his sons side with Willy against their father. Crucial in his struggle for influence is his disagreement with Willy and Diana in business matters. They call Wendy inestimably valuable and trustworthy, as if they, not Disson, were head of the firm. Trying to assert himself, Disson calls her 'not so bloody marvellous' but after a pause he admits she is 'all right' (III,121) – a defeat.

The play's structure derives from the increasing weakness of Disson and the increasing power of Willy, Diana, and Wendy. Against Disson's wishes, but conforming to Willy's former practice, Disson's sons call him 'sir' (III,112). Paradoxically Disson's excellent performance of an eye test further conveys his deteriorating psychological condition, for he admits that his sight erratically becomes unreliable. When Willy and Diana invite Wendy to join them on a trip to Spain, the trio seem to unite against Disson. Soon after, he imagines them in sexual activity and he collapses. His questions during his honeymoon, the sexual games he plays with Wendy, and the combination of sex, blindness, and power (Wendy, wrapping her chiffon scarf around his eyes, assumes control of him) suggest links between potency, sight, and authority; and his loss of one suggests loss of the others. The three areas merge when Willy and Disson's eye doctor take command of a sightless Disson who has fallen to the floor in his chair. 'Get him up', orders the occulist, and – a reference to the chair, but with sexual resonance – 'Get it up' (III,146).

The foregoing should not imply that the play lacks humour. To the contrary, its comedy of repetition even derives from sight, as when Disson's mother asks: 'Have I seen that mirror before?' 'No. It's new.' 'I knew I hadn't seen it' (III,138). Comedy also derives from incongruity (after praising the bride's taste and sensibility, Willy applauds her ability in competitive swimming), the unexpected (when Wendy explains that she left her previous job because her employer never stopped touching her, Disson asks, 'Where?' (III,105)), and double entendre (after Disson dictates a letter and then sexually manipulates Wendy, she reads back from her pad, 'There should be no difficulty in meeting your requirements' (III,117)).

Verbally and visually Pinter connects the play's scenes. Ironically Disson's dialogue in the first scene – 'You've heard of us' and 'I see' (III,103–4) – forecasts his inability to hear or see in the last scene when his wife asks if he can hear or see her. In an early scene Disson tells Willy that their offices are cut off from those of the other staff and from each other, and he asserts his dislike of fraternisation between offices. At the end of the play the blinded Disson is cut off from everyone and, immobile, cannot fraternise.

As in *The Collection*, infidelity is a subject of *The Homecoming*. As in *The Lover*, an unanticipated sexual arrangement concludes its action. As in *The Basement*, a woman's sexual allegiance shifts. As in *Tea Party*, a character who is unable to cope collapses. As in all these plays, but more savagely, characters in *The Homecoming* vie for positions of power, don protective masks, and both flippantly and abrasively mock each other.

To an all-male household – Max, a former butcher, his chauffeur brother Sam, and his sons Lenny and Joey, a pimp and a part-time boxer – the oldest son Teddy returns after six years in America, where he teaches philosophy, with his wife Ruth – a surprise to the family who did not know he had married or that he has three sons. At the end of the play the family proposes that Ruth stay, service them, and become a prostitute. After blurting out that Max's late wife Jessie committed adultery with his best friend, Sam collapses. Teddy leaves for America. Ruth remains.

In Act I the titular homecoming is Teddy's ('I was born here' (III,38)); in Act II Ruth's ('I was born quite near here' (III,69)). Even Act I hints at her homecoming. When she leaves for a solitary walk, Teddy gives her his key, which suggests possession. The title indicates a return not only to a house, but also to a state of being; a set of relationships, attitudes, and values; an ineluctable condition: 'Nothing's changed', in Teddy's words, 'Still the same' (III,38).

The play disorients. A butcher cooks what one of his sons calls dog food. A young fighter is knocked down by his old father. A philosopher refuses to philosophise. A chauffeur is unable to drive. A pimp takes orders from his whore. The whore does not go all the way with a man. Words disorient, as when Lenny says of Teddy, 'And my goodness we are proud of him here, I can tell you. Doctor of Philosophy and all that . . . leaves quite an impression' (III,47). The first phrase appropriate to an old woman not a young man, the triteness of the phrase that ends the first sentence, 'and all that' belittling the advanced degree – these disorient, thereby conveying the impression that what is said is not what is meant.

During the opening dialogue Lenny reads the racing section of a newspaper while Max asks for scissors and a cigarette. Although Max wants them, what underlies his requests is a demand for acknowledgement and attention. Lenny's indifference to his reminiscences, questions, insults, and threats indicates that the exchange is commonplace. Usually Lenny says nothing, a suggestion of his superior status (indeed, if he were not dominant, Max would not behave as he does). When Lenny speaks, it is often to assert a prerogative or to silence Max. When he initiates a subject (horseracing), it is to re-establish his status by contradicting Max, and when Max continues on it, Lenny's only response is to request a change of subject. Lenny takes the mickey out of Max who understands what Lenny is doing. When Max loses his temper and threatens to hit Lenny with his walking stick, Lenny mocks him by talking in a childlike manner. Beneath and through the dialogue they struggle for power – demanding recognition of status and self.

After the audience has seen Teddy's family, Teddy brings Ruth to the house. Before she meets them he describes them, first his father: 'I think you'll like him very much. Honestly.' From what we have seen, the statement is without foundation and Teddy's final adverb, designed to reassure Ruth, has a disconcerting effect on us, suggesting that he deliberately misleads. This suggestion intensifies when he describes them all as 'very warm people, really. Very warm. They're my family. They're not ogres'

(III,38–9). More imprecise than incongruous, the description is not technically a lie since warm means both affectionate (his suggestion) and passionate or heated (as they are in their hostilities); but, as before, Teddy misleads. If the reiterated 'very warm' or the overemphatic 'really' insufficiently indicates as much, then 'not ogres' should, for the family resembles ogres more than not ogres. The play confirms Teddy's deviousness. Before he married he did not introduce Ruth to his likeable father or very warm family who are not ogres, did not invite them to the wedding or even mention it (let alone his three sons), and he waits six years to surprise them with the news of his marriage. Alert to her husband's linguistic stratagems, Ruth refuses to reply. Since he waits a full page before he makes the second statement, he seems alert to her stratagems. Perhaps the devious Teddy did not introduce her to his family when they married but does so now because he expects to happen later what he expected to happen then. If this is the reason for his homecoming, a subtext helping to create the theatrical dynamics of this ambiguous play, it could underlie Pinter's statement (to John Lahr) 'that if ever there was a villain in the play, Teddy was it' and the identical words of Peter Hall and Paul Rogers (Max in Hall's production), that Teddy is 'the biggest bastard of the lot'.[4]

Ruth's encounter with Lenny, a struggle for domination, further reveals her proficiency at dealing with verbal stratagems. After she declines his offer of a refreshment, he says they do not have an alcoholic drink in the house. She does not respond, even with surprise, to his insult. Aware of his technique, she does not reveal hers. Trying another tactic, he says that she 'must be connected with' his brother. 'I'm his wife', she states (III,44). Immediately he changes the subject – another insult, to which, as before, she does not respond. Nor does she react to his sexual provocation,

which denies her status as his brother's wife: 'Isn't it funny?
I've got my pyjamas on and you're fully dressed.' Maliciously taunting her, he suggests she has left her husband
(he feigns surprise that both are in Europe), he speaks as if
she were his brother's mistress ('What, you sort of live with
him over there, do you?'), and he insinuates that the only
European sights she saw were bedroom walls ('On a visit to
Europe, eh? Seen much of it?'). Replying not to the underlying mockery but to the words on the surface, Ruth denies
him satisfaction and control. When he twice asks if he might
hold her hand, she twice, unruffled, asks why. By refusing
to respond in terms he dictates, she controls the situation. If
his story about hitting and kicking a syphilitic woman who
propositioned him shocks or worries her, she does not show
it but disconcertingly intimates, by asking him how he knew
the woman was diseased, that his violence does not concern
her. More subtly she insults him. When he says he has often
wished he were as sensitive as Teddy, she asks, 'Have you?'
(III,47). At the end of the scene she bullies him with the
same property he used to try to bully her: a glass of water
that, unasked, he gave her to drink. Now she refuses to
surrender it. When he threatens to take it, she threatens to
take him. Earlier he told her not to call him Leonard
because it is the name his mother gave him – implying that
she is not good enough to use it. Now she dominates by disregarding his order, and she demeaningly puts him in the
position of a child, inviting him to sit on her lap while he
sips, then while she pours water into his mouth, and commanding him to lie on the floor while she pours it down his
throat. Victoriously she laughs, drinks the water, smiles,
and leaves. He shouts after her. Whereas his taunts fail to
crack her cool demeanour, hers succeed in cracking his.

Max insults her further. After calling her a tart, a slut, a
scrubber, a whore, a slopbucket, a bedpan, and a disease,

and after striking two men, he commands her to come to him, maliciously calling her 'Miss'. Instead of leaving she maintains her mask and calmly approaches him – picking up a gauntlet without acknowledging that she does so. 'You a mother?' 'Yes.' 'How many you got?' 'Three.' (*He turns to* TEDDY.) 'All yours, Ted?' (III,59). Still she does not crack. This is the warmth Teddy promised, these the 'not ogres'.

Insults pervade the play, as do verbal violence (including a threat to chop someone's spine off and stories of beating women) and physical violence (Max hits Joey in the stomach and strikes Sam on the head with his stick). Although the power struggles are derisive and vicious, how strong are the characters? Peter Hall's 1965 production stressed menace and savagery. Kevin Billington's 1978 revival emphasised vulnerability and humanity. In Hall's interpretation a character's taunts charged the atmosphere with imminent violence or psychic destruction. In Billington's the weakness behind the mockery and the falseness of the bravado were so apparent, the challenger seemed to hope he would not have to make good his threat. In Hall's production Max's collapse after his brutal assault was a resting place while he gathered his considerable forces for the next struggle. In Billington's the momentary outburst took a greater toll on the weak old man, whose renewal required more effort.

Different viewpoints determine different performances. Lenny mocks his brother's profession. Apparently Teddy is an effete victim whom Lenny successfully taunts. Inquiring about his 'Doctorship of Philosophy', Lenny asks what he teaches. Is Teddy's reply – 'Philosophy' – straightforward or does he effectively mock the mocker? When Lenny, questioning him about the known and the unknown, calls it 'ridiculous to propose that what we *know* merits reverence', he implies that his brother, whom he knows, deserves no respect. Is Teddy caught short or does he coolly respond to the surface of the question, not the subtext? Since such questions are outside his province, he says, he is not the person to ask. Employing pseudo-philosophical locutions, Lenny presses his brother, who tries to maintain an air of calm detachment, but does he succeed? Perhaps Teddy is direct and effective (his statements are simple and clear), Lenny evasive and slow to reach the point ('Well, look at it this way' is a typical opening gambit) (III,68); but the actor playing Teddy might appear uncomfortable and the actor playing Lenny might speak his opening phrase maliciously.

After Teddy has packed his and Ruth's suitcases to return to America, Max proposes that she stay to service them. With a smile, Teddy suggests otherwise. Ignoring him, Max urges everyone to contribute to her maintenance. Still calm, Teddy refuses. Lenny suggests she earn her keep as a prostitute. When Max mockingly asks Teddy about her performance in bed, he responds as coolly as if the question concerned cornflakes. He remains detached when he hints to Ruth of his family's proposal and says nothing when they specify what they expect of her. Calmly Ruth negotiates terms. The power is hers, for no one else has the supply and everyone else has the demand. As Pinter says, 'She's misinterpreted deliberately and used by this family. But eventually she comes back at them with a whip. She says "if you want to play this game I can play it as well as you".'[5] According to Paul Rogers and John Normington (Sam in Hall's production), the outrageous setting-up of Ruth is an improvisation for the benefit of Teddy and Ruth and the astonishment of each other. When she takes them seriously, perhaps setting them up, they are hoist by their own petard.[6] Only one character drops his mask of detachment,

Sam, who blurts out that Jessie cuckolded Max and then falls to the floor. The accusation fails to disturb Max, whose only response is to call Sam's imagination diseased, and the collapse merely incommodes Teddy, who must find another ride to the airport. Sam's behaviour highlights the fact that no one else betrays emotion. With studied calm, Teddy bids the men goodbye and accepts a photograph of Max for his grandchildren. With equal calculation, he does not speak to his wife. When she sluttishly tells him not to become a stranger, thereby mocking him, he leaves without a word, thereby mocking her.

Although the play is savage, it is comic too – often at the same time. Incongruity combines with derision when Max peers at Ruth's face as she lies beneath Joey, then tells her husband she is 'a woman of quality' (III,76). Lighter mockery underlies comic tautology, as in Lenny's response to Sam's statement that he took an American to the airport: 'Had to catch a plane there, did he?' (III,28). Comic repetition is part of power struggles, as in an exchange between Ruth and Teddy: 'Can I sit down?' 'Of course.' 'I'm tired.' 'Then sit down' (III,36). The unexpected literalisation of a figure of speech underscores a power struggle: 'Shall I go up and see if my room's still there?' 'It can't have moved' (III,36).

Verbally Pinter connects sequences of *The Homecoming*. In Act I Lenny talks of having perhaps been a soldier in the Italian campaign during World War II; in Act II Ruth mentions having perhaps been a nurse in that campaign. In Act I Max taunts Sam about taking a wife and bringing her home, where she can make them all happy; in Act II he and Lenny propose this to Teddy and his wife. Before Sam's second act accusation, he hints in the first act that Jessie may have been what Ruth might become, a prostitute. He calls Jessie charming, but he adds an unusual reservation:

'All the same, she was your wife.' His driving her about town gave him 'some of the most delightful evenings I've ever had', he remembers with nostalgia and vindictiveness. Although he does not call her a prostitute, Max's response indicates disturbance at Sam's pleasure: '(*softly, closing his eyes*) Christ' (III,31–2). Max's seemingly unfavourable comparison of Ruth with Jessie actually demonstrates that he regards both women the same way. After Teddy exclaims that Ruth is his wife, Max pauses – suggestive of careful consideration – and then links, as he apparently contrasts, the women: 'I've never had a whore under this roof before. Ever since your mother died' (III,58).

Parallel actions abound. Each act ends with Max asking for affection – first from Teddy, then from Ruth. In Act I Teddy brings Ruth to his former home; in Act II he leaves her there. When Lenny meets her, he asks what she might want; at the end she gives specifications. Joey's first action concerning her is a refusal to throw her out; at the end she pats his head. When Max first sees her, he ignores her; at the end she does not respond to him. In the first scene Max admits he is getting old; in the last he denies it.

Visually past exists in present. The set shows that '*The back wall, which contained the door, has been removed. A square arch shape remains. Beyond it, the hall*' (III,21). When Teddy and Ruth enter, he calls her attention to the arch. John Bury's set for Peter Hall's production was selectively realistic, not naturalistic. The staircase, much larger than an actual one, ascended above the proscenium arch. The setting was stark, suggestive of coldness, hostility, a house wherein no affection could exist. By contrast Eileen Diss's setting for Kevin Billington's production was naturalistic. She even showed the second storey, with characters entering and leaving bedrooms. Savagery and violence, her set suggested, are not strange but exist in a home-like environment, familiar to the audience.

Without words Pinter conveys attitudes. After Ruth leaves, Teddy goes to the window at stage right and peers out, watching her. Lenny enters from upstage left and stands there. Teddy turns to see him. The meaning of their words conveys little. The stage picture conveys a great deal: although the brothers have not seen each other for six years, they do not move for almost two pages but regard each other from opposite sides of the stage. Throughout they neither embrace nor shake hands. Moreover this scene occurs after Teddy tells Ruth his family is very warm; it comments ironically on that statement and reveals the brothers' relationship – scrutinising and testing, as if before a fight. When Teddy picks up his and Ruth's suitcases, Lenny offers to give him a hand but does not move. Only after Teddy has gone into the hall and Lenny turned out the light does he follow his brother to ask if he wants anything. By then the question is clearly *pro forma*.

In the second scene between Ruth and Lenny she makes an overture to him (asking what he thinks of her shoes), in contrast to his overtures in their first scene. In the University of Calgary production Richard Hornby suggestively visualised this by placing Ruth on a sofa and Lenny on a footstool facing her. Thus, says Hornby, Ruth showed him not only her shoe but also a bit of her leg. 'Lenny, as he said, "They're very nice", let his eyes travel from her feet up her legs, so that it was not quite clear to which he was referring. Continuing to turn her foot and look at it, Ruth delivered her next line, "No, I can't get the ones I want over there", with a kind of *over*casualness.' By slightly over-emphasising 'them' Lenny agreed that footwear was not all she could not get in America. As she concurred their eyes made contact for the first time, confirming that they recognised the subject was more than shoes. Yet 'it was all done in a simple and understated manner'.[7]

The final stage picture portrays the ambiguous note on which the play ends. Previously Ruth preferred not to finalise the proposed agreement but to negotiate details later. At the end of the play she sits enthroned, with Joey's head in her lap and Max on his knees before her in supplication. Lenny stands apart, mutely and perhaps obediently watching. Possibly Ruth will control the men rather than be controlled by them, but Lenny's silence – maintained, like Ruth's, since bidding Teddy goodbye – may indicate his control, and standing is usually a stronger stage position than sitting or kneeling, particularly here, where Lenny is upstage of and at a distance from the cluster of mistress and attendants. Whatever one may infer from her victory over him in their first scene together is balanced by her taking the initiative in their second. Because Ruth has yet to work out final terms with a man whose profession is pimp, the play's end – notwithstanding his previous agreement to her demands – is ambiguous.

In their frequently vicious struggles for power, no character is clearly victorious. Does Teddy intend at the start to let the nature of his family take its course and claim Ruth? If so, or if not, he does not leave the London house unscarred. Is Ruth at the end in the position of Queen Bee? If so, she may for specified periods of time become a worker who supports the drones.

6
Memory Plays

In most of Pinter's plays the past is unclear: Stanley's trans-gression (*The Birthday Party*), Aston's experience in the mental asylum (*The Caretaker*), adultery (*The Collection*), and so forth. More prominently than before, however, the works treated in this chapter focus on the past. Usually they are called memory plays.

Landscape has two characters, Beth and Duff, who live in the house of their former employer, apparently deceased. They reminisce. Her memories include the sea, the beach, and a man lying on a sand dune; his, a dog, a park, and a pub. Her memories are gentle and fragile; his, frequently vulgar and aggressive. They do not converse with each other.

Like a painting, *Landscape* contains no movement. The characters do not leave their chairs, which a kitchen table separates; and they are separated from their background, which is dim. Figuratively the stage picture is an immobile landscape. The vista is distant, in that the audience is unable to penetrate beneath the facades of the reminiscing

85

characters. Despite the clarity of the figures in the fore-
ground, the sketch is faint and shadowy.

What happens, what the audience perceives, is two characters, physically and emotionally separated from each
other and their environment, dwelling on their memories.
Almost at the outset, Pinter hints that these memories may
not be reliable. Beth recalls: 'Two women looked at me,
turned and stared. No. I was walking, they were still. I
turned' (III,178). The man on the beach, whom she fondly
remembers, may be Duff or their employer, or her memory
may fuse both.

In a stage direction, Pinter states that while Duff normally refers to Beth, she never looks at him, and that each '*does
not appear to hear*' the other's voice (III,175). This differs
from not hearing, which Pinter would have said if it were
what he meant. Not only does their attitude suggest
estrangement, it also suggests habitual estrangement, for
Duff seems unsurprised when Beth does not answer his
questions. He tries to engage her in conversation. When he
proposes they walk to the pond, she pauses but does not
reply. When he contritely recalls his earlier confession of
infidelity, she changes the subject. Conciliatory, he asks
whether she likes him to talk to her and though she is unre-
sponsive he tries to maintain an illusion of *rapport*: 'I think
you do' (III,189).

Subtly Pinter suggests that she hears him. A moment
after he says there was no one in the park, she says there
was no one on the beach; he mentions a pub, she a hotel
bar. Perhaps because each is persistent – he demanding
acknowledgement, she refusing to give it – hostilities
develop. After he recalls that she infrequently laughed and
was grave, she remembers when she laughed and smiled.
When he talks of himself, she recalls an unnamed, gentle
man beside whom she lay down. Her memories of beautiful

moments prompt, perhaps in retaliation, vulgarity, such as references to 'Dogshit, duckshit, all kinds of shit' (III,180) – and it is noteworthy that the only comedy in this play is, atypically for Pinter, that of obscenity. Although Duff does not say that Beth's uncommunicativeness increasingly angers him, he conveys as much. When his statement that what really matters is that they are together is met first by silence, then by a change of subject, he, thus rejected, changes the subject again and becomes more vulgar; and he talks of brutally making love to her in front of the dog and against a hanging gong. Instead of acknowledging his prov-ocation, she retaliates by remembering tender amative-ness.

Two incompatible people, once loving, are isolated from each other, implicitly rejecting each other, uncommuni-cative in an unchanging landscape. The play's final line, spoken by Beth, is ambiguous, 'Oh my true love I said' (III,198) – apparently tender, but invoking a past love and thereby rejecting the man presently near her, as his verbal rape had just demeaned her.

As in *Landscape*, the noncomic *Silence* situates each of its characters in a chair in a distinct area of the stage – visually symbolic of isolation. Unlike *Landscape*, a charac-ter occasionally moves to another character. What the three personae of *Silence* remember occurred when Rum-sey was forty, Bates in his mid-thirties, and Ellen in her twenties – their ages as they appear on stage.

Rumsey lives in the country, and when Ellen wanted to marry him he urged her to find a younger man. But she rejected Bates, who is associated with the city and traffic. Now, living apart, they reminisce, and they repeat their recollections, but with ellipses. For example, the play begins, 'I walk with my girl who wears a grey blouse when she walks and grey shoes and walks with me readily wearing her clothes considered for me. Her grey clothes'; in two later sequences, the same character remembers, 'I walk with my girl who wears –' (III,201,214). The effect differs considerably from that of *The Dumb Waiter*, in which responses to newspaper stories are repeated but without the stories themselves. In *The Dumb Waiter*, the effect is menace; in *Silence*, fading memory. Early in the play, Ellen candidly states that she is never sure of when her memories took place or how much she really recalls. Then, apparently exasperated by her drinking companion's continual questioning of whether she had been married, she finally says, 'Certainly. I can remember the wedding' (III,214). In a recapitulatory closing segment, she mentions neither uncertain memories nor badgering friend but only repeats the statement quoted.

All three characters, having chosen solitary lives, remember the past when they were together. Silences often separate their mnemonic monologues that decreasingly dovetail each other, until after a long silence that concludes the play, memory seems to fade with the fading lights. Like *Landscape, Silence* is a verbal construct with minimal action and character interrelations – a recited piece, more poetic than dramatic.

Much shorter than either is *Night*, another memory play with no movement but, unlike the others, with a conventional story. Also unlike them, it is generally comic and unlike other Pinter plays has a celebratory conclusion. A married couple, both in their forties, have conflicting memories of their first stroll together. They stood by the railings of a field, says she; on a bridge, says he. But they agree on how they met and loved each other. Their bickering is amusing, not malicious. Although he remembers standing behind her and touching her breasts, she is puzzled: 'But my back was against railings. [. . .] You were facing me' (III,226). Such details are unimportant. They agree that he had had her and had said he loved her and would always adore her. They also agree that he still adores her. 'Gentle' and 'sweet' are adjectives one does not usually apply to Pinter's plays, but both befit the lovely *Night*, wherein the past brings nostalgia, not dread. Pinter goes gently into *Night*.

These atypical works, however, seem to be experiments in craft and strengthenings of thematic concepts to be employed in a major work in which memory is prominent. Pinter's next play is that work, *Old Times*, written six years after *The Homecoming*, his last previous full-length play. In between, apart from the three plays just discussed, he wrote screenplays that may have affected *Old Times*. A subject of *The Quiller Memorandum* is a political ideology of an older time, Nazism, which characters remember and try to revive. *Accident* is told in flashbacks, which show old times. *Old Times* has a namesake in *Accident*, Anna, and each Anna is associated with a country other than England: the movie's is an Austrian princess, the play's lives in Sardinia. The start of *The Go-Between*, also about memory, repeats L. P. Hartley's evocative 'The past is a foreign country. They do things differently there.'[1] As in *Accident, Old Times* has a namesake in *The Go-Between*: a minor character named Kate. Perhaps Pinter uses these names to pay homage to the novels from which the films derive. Cinema occupies a more prominent role in *Old Times* than in any of his other plays: two characters talk of *Odd Man Out* and one says he directs movies.

In *Old Times*, Deeley and Kate, married, live on the seacoast. Anna, a former roommate of Kate's, visits them. The women reminisce. Later, Deeley and Anna say they met each other twenty years before. Their rivalry over Kate intensifies. Kate, asserting her dominant position, terminates their sparring. As terms like rivalry and sparring suggest, the stratagems, taunts, and power struggles that characterise plays like *The Collection* and *The Homecoming*, where the past is also important, are major factors in this play.

Characters in *Old Times* discuss old times, such as what the women did and whom they saw when they were roommates, the first meeting between husband and wife, and a flirtation at a party. They even sing old songs. Anna's opening speech is a profusion of memories. At the play's outset, the other two try to pin down the past. Is Anna thin or fat? 'Fuller than me', says Kate, and adds, 'I think' (7). Memory is unreliable. Paradoxically, it contains its own validity. As Anna says, one may sometimes remember what never happened, but *as* one recalls events, they do happen. In the play, characters remember or imagine time past, which they discuss, sometimes enact or re-enact, in time present.

Underlying what happens after Anna arrives is an earlier exchange between Deeley and Kate: 'Are you looking forward to seeing her?' 'No' (11). Kate's response suggests how the actresses might play the roles, and how Mary Ure and Rosemary Harris did, in Peter Hall's New York production – Ure (Kate) polite, reserved, not outgoing; Harris (Anna) outgoing and friendly. Anna's effusive first speech, about her and Kate's past, covers almost a page. Kate does not immediately respond, and when she does she is laconic, 'Yes, I remember' (18), then is silent for over a page. In Act I, moreover, it is Anna, not Kate, who takes the initiative in discussing their old times in London. In Act II, however, after Kate's marriage is revealed as less happy than the opening suggests, both women take the initiative.

Memories arouse rivalry and battles for domination through participation in a past or through one's ability to persuade another to accept an interpretation of it. Early, when Deeley asks if Anna were Kate's best friend, Kate avoids answering. When he persists, she calls Anna her only friend, explaining, 'If you have only one of something, you can't say it's the best of anything' (9). It is he who accepts her interpretation. Because knowledge means power, memory is a weapon. Anna's recollection of her and Kate's activities in London excludes Deeley. His remembrance of meeting Kate at a showing of *Odd Man Out* excludes her. He may try to usurp Anna's past by usurping her diction – 'gaze', which he says is infrequently used; she may try to usurp his memory when she talks of seeing *Odd Man Out* with Kate (though both stories may be true: after having met Deeley at the cinema where it played, Kate could have returned with Anna).

From the start, Deeley is hostile toward Anna. After her opening speech about old times in London is a '*Slight pause*' before he insists on Kate's different present life: 'We rarely get to London' (18). Kate pours coffee for all. Perhaps as alternative, Deeley pours brandy for all. In the text, he pours himself another two pages later and one fifteen pages after that. In the New York production, Robert Shaw continued to hold the bottle after the second drink. Increasing inebriation underlay increasing aggressiveness. Taking his measure, Rosemary Harris's taunts were so subtle as to validate her later denial of hostility.

Deeley's suspicion that Kate and Anna were lesbians may derive solely from his insecurities, which might also prompt his recollection of lesbian usherettes in the cinema. When he labels their former life together a marriage, Anna responds, 'We were great friends.' When he inquires about Kate's passion, she answers, 'I feel that is your province.' When he calls the subject of their former life distasteful, Anna asks why and reminds him that she has flown from Italy to see her oldest friend and to meet him. Soon, she says she 'came here not to disrupt but to celebrate [. . .] a very old and treasured friendship, something that was forged between us long before you knew of our existence' (66–8). Yet her last phrase undercuts her reassurance, for the celebration excludes him.

Deeley's recollection of seeing *Odd Man Out*, part of his struggle with Anna, excludes her from a shared experience with Kate; it deprecates her by a reference to an usherette who achieved sexual satisfaction by stroking her breasts (Anna is temporarily husbandless), simultaneously flirting with another usherettè (as he perceives she does with Kate); and it indirectly warns her that she cannot destroy his marriage: 'So it was Robert Newton who brought us together and it is only Robert Newton who can tear us apart.' After a pause, Anna – perhaps recognising his stratagem – indicates, by trying to undermine his frame of reference, that one might be able to do so: 'F. J. McCormick was good too.' He may recognise her stratagem, for he reasserts his premise: 'I know F. J. McCormick was good too. But he didn't bring us together' (30).

Their song-competition in the first act stems from rivalry over Kate. With one exception, the accompanying stage direction is '*Singing*' (27–8). The exception is the first: Deeley sings '*to* KATE'. She is the prize to be won. In the second-act reprise, Kate turns to look at them and after four lines of song, she walks toward them and stands, smiling. They '*sing again, faster on cue, and more perfunctorily*' (58). Kate, not song, is their focal point.

In Act I, Deeley sings the opening lines of 'Lovely to Look At' and 'Blue Moon', suggesting that he and not Anna knows his lovely wife, who delights him, and that she like the blue moon stood alone, unattached, when he first saw her. Changing songs, a riposte, Anna begins, 'They Can't Take That Away from Me', but though she sings the first line, Deeley interrupts to sing the last, its title. Anna again changes songs. Starting 'The Way You Look Tonight', she hints that Kate looks lovely for *her* sake, but Deeley interrupts, suggesting that he has a woman crazy for *him*. Defeated again, Anna changes songs again. As before, she begins the stanza but Deeley concludes it, to assert that all the things Kate is are *his*. Anna sings four lines of another song, but Deeley tops her with the fifth, title line, that *he* gets a kick out of Kate. In another song change, Anna indicates that *her* true love was true, since one cannot deny something inside. Deeley interrupts her, but she interrupts him with the final, titular line, which throws smoke in Deeley's eyes. Outmaneouvred he begins 'These Foolish Things Remind Me of You.' Each sings a line, and the song stops before it ends, with neither a clear-cut victor. In Act II, they have another song-competition, this time not a medley but one song, 'They Can't Take That Away from Me', whose final, title line Anna sings at the end of the first stanza but Deeley sings at the end of the second; at the close of the third, stepping from performance to reality, he speaks it, a possible suggestion that he is victorious.

Like Ruth in *The Homecoming*, the woman who is want-ed can control those who want her. Anna requires confir-mation of past and therefore of self, and her long opening speech is sprinkled with questions appended to assertions, such as 'Queuing all night, the rain, do you remember?' and 'to a concert, or the opera, or the ballet, that night, you haven't forgotten?' (17). By contrast the independent Kate requires no confirmation by another person.

As Deeley and Anna recognise, Kate is the vital force of this trio. Denying Kate's charge that she considered her dead, Anna calls her 'animated' (34). Deeley agrees that Kate's vivacity and vitality are more than the word 'animated suggests. To the reader the agreement may seem odd, for so far Kate has taken little part in the conversation. In production, however – certainly in Mary Ure's performance – the agreement was apt, for the actress had been, though relatively silent, an alert, dominant presence. Later her strength and self-reliance become more evident. Anna and Deeley discuss which of them should dry Kate when she completes her bath, but their debate is irrelevant: when Kate enters, she has already dried herself. For self fulfilment they need her, not she them.

Anna's apparent victory in the first act is chiefly by default. After Deeley derides Kate as someone he saddled himself with twenty years earlier and whose sole claim to virtue was her silence, after he refers to her with demeaning clichés, as if she were his to command – 'Well, any time your husband finds himself in this direction my little wife will be only too glad to put the old pot on the old gas stove' (41) – and after he thrice interrupts her conversation with Anna by talking about himself, Kate takes sides. Unexpectedly Anna refers to old times as if she and Kate were still in London. More unexpectedly Kate joins her in converting past into present, thereby excluding Deeley.

Although Kate also appears to side against Deeley at the end of the second act (she tells him that if he does not like her conversation with Anna he can leave), she seems to relent after Anna claims credit for making Kate's London years so happy: 'I found her. She grew to know wonderful people, through my introduction. I took her to cafes' (69). Responding to Anna's false step, Deeley tells Kate he had met Anna twenty years before. He tries to deny Anna's identity. She pretended to be Kate, he says, let him look at the underwear she wore, which was Kate's. 'She thought she was you, said little, said little. Maybe she was you. Maybe it was you.' Kate tells him that this woman, who might have been she, was attracted to his sensitive, vulnerable face and fell in love with him. When Anna, trying to regain command, insists it was her skirt, not Kate's, up which Deeley looked, Kate destroys her. Whereas Anna tells Deeley she remembers him, Kate tells her, 'I remember you dead.' More than dead, Kate adds, Anna never really existed for her. When Deeley asked who slept in the other bed in the apartment, she told him, 'No one at all' (69–73). In Act I, Kate dispossesses Deeley; in Act II, Anna, and the latter is more final. Yet Kate, not Deeley, is the victor, and she dictates terms. Retaining her independence, she takes him as a ruler would a subject. As for marrying him instead of throwing dirt on his face, as she did on Anna's, she says it did not matter. She has the power to devitalise him. While Deeley triumphs over Anna, it is through Kate, who triumphs over both.

This discussion of death, however, should not obscure the play's comedy, some of which derives from de-animation, such as: 'You have a wonderful casserole.' 'What?' 'I mean wife' (20). Some is based on sarcasm, as Kate's response to Deeley's surprise that she and Anna lived together: 'Of course we did. How else would she steal my underwear from me? In the street?' (17). Some comes from the mockery that accompanies rivalry, as the exchange between Deeley and Anna: 'I've got a brilliant idea. Why don't we [dry Kate] with powder?' 'Is that a brilliant idea?' (56). And there is the humour that derives from the familiar Pinter techniques of repetition, tautology, and incongruity.

Verbally and visually, sequences connect. In Act I, Deeley disparages Kate as 'a trueblue pickup' (30); in Act II, he disparages Anna when he says that in permitting him a view up her skirt at Kate's underwear, which she wore, she displayed 'Trueblue generosity' (69). In Act I, Kate

reprimands Anna for talking of her as if she were dead; in
Act II, she remembers Anna as dead. An important link is
between Anna's first-act story of the crying man and the
play's conclusion, which dramatises the story. Anna
remembers returning to her room one night to find a man
sitting crumbled in the armchair, sobbing, his hand over his
face, and Kate sitting on the bed with a mug of coffee.
Neither spoke to her or looked up. She undressed, turned
off the light, and got into her bed. The man slowly walked
toward her and stopped in the centre of the room. He
looked at her and Kate, then turned toward her,
approached her bed, and bent down over her. After a time,
she heard him leave, but later in the night she awakened
and saw two shapes on Kate's bed. He lay across Kate's lap.
By early morning he had gone. Three points are noteworthy: first, Anna's recollection directly follows her statement that what she remembers might not have happened
but does happen as she recalls it; second, the re-enactment
occurs well after she recalls it; third, it does not follow her
story in every detail. The major difference is the conclusion. To Anna, the man's departure the next morning
denied his presence the previous night: 'It was as if he had
never been.' Deeley disputes this interpretation: 'Of course
he'd been. He went twice and came once' (33). In the
re-enactment, Deeley does not even depart once. Anna
does not *make* her real or false memory take place. In her
memory, the dispossessed man is annihilated; just before
the re-enactment, however, Kate annihilates Anna and
denies her former presence (in her bed). Neither marriage
nor a change of environment mattered to Kate then, she
says, but while her concluding words subdue Deeley, they
demolish Anna.

Pinter's visual imagery reflects his themes. During the
first song-competition, Kate sits while Anna and Deeley

stand. They are engaged, she detached; they performers, she the spectator each tries to please. The divans and arm-chairs of Act II are in exactly the same relationship to each other as the sofas and armchair of Act I, but in reversed positions – reflective of the reversed positions of Anna and Deeley toward Kate. At the start of Act I, Deeley and Kate discuss Anna, who stands, back toward them, in dim light, as the past is a dim presence with the potential to emerge, which she does. At the start of Act II, Anna is alone, but any idea that the room is hers vanishes when Deeley enters and explains the furniture arrangement: her possession is apparent, not real. The presence of the absent member of the trio is indicated not by that person standing in dim light, but by a faint glow from the glass panel of the bathroom door. When Kate enters, she walks to the window and, like Anna in Act I, stands for a time with her back to the others.

Although dim light opens the play, whose first word is 'Dark' (7), a reference to Anna's complexion, a blaze of bright light ends it. The contrasting lighting intensities imply contrasting modes of consciousness, dim and full. The different tableaux, as well as the different lighting, point to change. Anna stands at the start, lies down at the end. Kate is curled on a sofa at the start, sits on a divan at the end. From standing to lying down is a considerable difference, and Anna's radically altered image suggests that of the three characters her downfall is the most extreme change; the glaring light of consciousness makes it more ignominious still. From a curling to an upright posi-tion, Kate emerges triumphant and more aware of her power. That Deeley has the same posture (slumped in an armchair) would indicate that while his position is no differ-ent, his consciousness of it is fuller. The closing tableau shows rejection (Anna), power (Kate), and return or reun-ion without triumph (Deeley).

Like *Landscape* and *Silence, Old Times* is a memory play, but unlike these plays, *Old Times* portrays, in terms of dramatic conflict, the past's influence on the present. Unlike *Night*, which also contains conflict, the resolution of *Old Times* is devastating – akin, in this respect, to that of the other full-length plays thus far analysed.

7
Recapitulations and Fresh Starts

In certain respects, to be explored below, Pinter's most recent plays recapitulate earlier themes and techniques. In other respects, also to be examined, they move – sometimes provisionally, sometimes boldly – in new directions. With *Monologue* and *No Man's Land*, the familiar terrain is more obvious than the new; with *Betrayal*, the reverse.

Old Times deals with two former female friends and a man; *Monologue*, with two former male friends and a woman. Before the start of *Monologue*, a woman whom the speaker loved left him for his friend. The woman is black, the male friends white. The speaker has not seen the couple recently (how long is unclear, though long enough for them to have had more than one child). Asserting his friendship with the man and his fondness of both, he hopes for readmission to their company.

Monologue is a monologue. Its meaning inheres in its title. In drama, a monologue refers to a solitary person speaking, but not to himself, as in a soliloquy, and it differs from dialogue. In *Monologue*, a solitary character talks, but not to himself. The title is also apt in that the play is about isolation, its speaker is alone from start to finish, and no dialogue or response is possible. Because Pinter employs the visual as well as the verbal, *Monologue* can be effective only when an audience sees the play, not simply hears it recited: the speaker talks to an empty chair. Whereas Eugene Ionesco uses many chairs, in his play *The Chairs*, to embody nothingness and to suggest the metaphysical void, Pinter in *Monologue* employs one empty chair to embody absence and to suggest the isolation and loneliness of the play's sole character. The stage picture – a man addressing an empty chair – is a concrete, theatrical metaphor of the subject.

The play's ambience is the subtle, tragicomic movement from friendship to loneliness, as the speaker increasingly reveals the depths of his affection for the man and love for the woman. In losing her, he also lost him, and he pleads for their friendship, offering to die for their children, if they have children. But an empty chair cannot respond. At the end of the play, he fully reveals his true isolation and loneliness.

Yet the start is comic. Pinter even parodies the nature of a monologue. After two pages, including half-a-dozen questions to the empty chair, the speaker pauses and observes ironically, 'The thing I like, I mean quite immeasurably, is this kind of conversation, this kind of exchange, this class of mutual reminiscence.' Comedy also derives from exaggeration and repetition: 'I've got a hundred per cent more energy in me now than when I was twenty-two. When I was twenty-two I slept twenty-four hours a day. And twenty-two hours at twenty-four. Work it out for yourself.'

Pinter forges verbal and thematic links. At the start, the speaker suggests a game of ping pong with his friend; after revealing their rivalry, he says, 'You're not even ready for a game of ping pong.' At first, 'black' is a term of mockery. The speaker says that while his friend looked bold in black, he did not like his face, which was too white between black hair and black jacket. He concludes, 'you should have had a black face'. By the end, when he repeats the quoted phrase, the mockery turns against the speaker. The verbal wit that accompanies apparent self-assurance at the start becomes verbal desperation at the end, as the speaker, lacking real assurance, recognises his loneliness.

Like *The Dwarfs*, *Monologue* concerns the deterioration of friendship. Len and the speaker, both preoccupied with arithmetic, are at the end isolated from their friends; yet the speaker's isolation is less ambiguous than that of Len, who has some comfort in cleanliness and foliage. As in *The Basement*, a woman changes her affection from a man to his friend, but *Monologue* forecasts no reverse dramatic movement for the castaway friend. The triangle of *The Homecoming* contains a man, his wife, and his male relatives; it ends shortly after the man's departure and does not portray his attitude years after the woman has rejected him. By contrast, *Monologue* does. Such open display of emotion is uncommon in the Pinter canon. But the speaker is safe in dropping his mask and revealing his solitude, emptiness, and vulnerability. He confronts only an empty chair. He is utterly alone.

Many of Pinter's plays concern an intruder or outsider, plus a group or couple intruded upon or visited by the outsider. At the end, someone leaves or is about to go. In *The Caretaker* it is the intruder; in *A Slight Ache*, one of the couple who receives the visitor. When the dispossessed figure is forced to go, his expulsion is psychologically overwhelming. Unique among Pinter's plays that contain this theme, the action of *Monologue* occurs after expulsion.

Whereas expulsion is the climax of the major action in other works, although dispossession may have occurred in previous situations, it is exclusively expository in *Monologue*. Thus Pinter permits the audience to see, more clearly than elsewhere, the consequences, the suffering face beneath the mask.

Although *No Man's Land* contains more than one character, its opening is almost a monologue by the garrulous Spooner, a down-at-heel, self-styled poet whom Hirst, a famous, prosperous writer, meets and brings home for a drink. Spooner attempts to ingratiate himself with his host and thereby to install himself in Hirst's home, replacing Foster and Briggs who are employed to protect Hirst from outside encroachment. Spooner's efforts fail.

In Act I, Hirst states and explains the titular phrase: 'No man's land . . . does not move . . . or change . . . or grow old . . . remains . . . forever . . . icy . . . silent' (34). In Act II, Spooner does the same, with changes that emphasise finality: it 'never moves' and 'never changes' (95). In an alcoholic haze, Hirst remains, secured by Foster and Briggs against intruders who might alter his life, and Spooner is forever excluded from the haven he seeks.

What Spooner tries to do is what Foster warns against: 'drive a wedge into a happy household' (50). Foster and Briggs try to disorient the stranger who threatens their position. Although Foster's initial words are 'What are you drinking?' his pressing question – 'Who are you?' – is balanced by such taunts as 'Have you met your host?' (35). The conclusion of Act I encapsulates the menace directed against Spooner. Quietly Foster tells him, 'You know what it's like when you're in a room with the light on and then suddenly the light goes out? I'll show you. It's like this.' He then turns out the light, darkening the stage (53). Briggs is more overtly threatening. Making no effort to conceal his malice, he refers to Spooner as 'a pisshole collector', 'a shit-house operator', 'a jamrag vendor', 'a mingejuice bottler, a fucking shitcake baker' (88). His sometimes superficial affability does not deceive Spooner, who calls his 'offer of alms' (breakfast) the equivalent of 'The shark in the harbour' (60). He and Briggs take the piss out of each other: 'I am a poet.' 'I thought poets were young.' 'I am young' (63–4).

The relationship between Spooner and Hirst is ambiguous. They may have known each other years ago, each may have confused the other with someone else, Spooner may lie in order to establish a basis for friendship, or all may be true, but at different times. This uncertainty creates an aura of mystery.

At times, the mystery is comic, as in the inversion that terminates one of their recollections:

> I was terribly fond of Bunty. He was most dreadfully annoyed with you. Wanted to punch you in the nose.
> What for?
> For seducing his sister.
> What business was it of his?
> He was her brother.
> That's my point (73).

When Spooner remembers sharing a drink with someone, Hirst unexpectedly asks, turning the figurative into the literal, 'The same drink?' (23). Comic repetition connects to memory, as when Spooner says, 'And I wonder at you, now, as once I wondered at him. But will I wonder at you tomorrow, I wonder, as still I wonder at him today?' (26). Much of the mockery is funny, including Foster's references to Spooner, who calls himself a friend of the host, as Mr Friend.

Through words and attitudes, Pinter connects scenes. As mentioned, each act contains an explanation of the title. The opening lines presage the conclusion. 'As it is?' asks Hirst, referring to whisky. 'As it is', affirms Spooner, 'yes please absolutely as it is' (15). Although the concluding lines do not repeat the phrase, they suggest it, for after Spooner explains the unchanging nature of no man's land, in which everything remains absolutely as it is, Hirst proposes to drink to that, and he does so. In Act I, after a short nap, Hirst wonders who was drowning in his dream. Spooner claims it was he. In Act II, Hirst gratuitously refers to the dream in order to reject Spooner's bid: 'I say to myself, I saw a body, drowning. But I am mistaken. There is nothing there' (95). At the start, two old men are friendly; at the end, estranged – one immobilised like the photographs in his album, the other evicted from a haven of food, drink, and companionship.

No Man's Land may be the end of a phase in Pinter's writing, for it echoes many of his previous works. The ambience of menace recalls the early plays, and some of the menace is comic. Struggles for power between Spooner and Hirst's aides recall the works that focus on this theme, and as in those plays mockery is sometimes funny, sometimes threatening. The mutual reminiscences of Spooner and Hirst recall the memory plays. *No Man's Land* echoes specific works as well as groups: *The Birthday Party* (the stage suddenly plunged into darkness), *The Hothouse* (a character unexpectedly left alone in a room), *A Slight Ache* (a loquacious character who says that a silent or laconic one is reticent), *The Caretaker* (a seedy visitor who fails to establish himself as a mainstay in a benefactor's home), *The Collection* (homosexuality), *Tea Party* (the boastful self-appraisal of an insecure character which proves hollow), *The Homecoming* (malicious taunting beneath a veneer of affability), and *Old Times* (the unreliability of memory). Foster's reference to Spooner's effort to disrupt a happy household suggests several earlier plays, including *The Collection, The Homecoming*, and *Old Times*.

Yet *No Man's Land* sounds new notes as well as old. More than in any previous play by Pinter, one is aware of wealth. The setting bespeaks it: an antique liquor cabinet, a book-lined wall, and heavy curtains across an expanse of upstage windows. Hirst's wealth, on which Foster comments, is particularly evident because it contrasts with Spooner's poverty. Whereas Hirst's clothes are expensive, Spooner's are old and shabby. The contrast between Spooner's language and his appearance reveals him as *dé classé*. Whereas he has been downwardly mobile, Foster and Briggs have been upwardly mobile – contrasting declassment. The same year Pinter wrote *No Man's Land*, 1974, he completed his film adaptation of F. Scott Fitzgerald's *The Last Tycoon*, whose subjects include wealthy, upwardly declassed film-makers.

Another subject of *The Last Tycoon* is the artist. *No Man's Land* is populated with artists and – apart from *A Slight Ache*, whose protagonist writes essays but not poetry, fiction, or drama – is Pinter's first play to deal directly with people in his own profession: writers. Three of the four characters are or claim to be poets (Hirst, Spooner, and Foster), as Pinter is. Usually Pinter displaces his profession by creating different types of artists. In *The Birthday Party* Stanley may have been a pianist. Pinter is also an actor, but the actors mentioned in *The Dwarfs* remain offstage. *The Collection* has dress designers, not writers. *The Lover* features improvisations (an acting technique) by characters who are not actors. In *The Homecoming* Ruth says she was a model for the body, which may mean either prostitute or real model (a displacement of the actor). In

Old Times Deeley may be what he says he is, a movie director (Pinter, who directs plays, did not direct a film until after he wrote this play). In *No Man's Land*, however, Pinter deals directly with creative writers.

Although writers and writing are among the subjects of *Betrayal*, no writer appears on stage. Instead writers' surrogates appear: a literary agent and a publisher (Jerry and Robert). They and Emma (the latter's wife, the former's mistress) discuss real writers past – Ford Madox Ford and W. B. Yeats – and fictitious writers present, especially Casey, a striking offstage presence. At one point he has left his wife and three children and is writing a novel of a man who has left his wife and three children – whereas an earlier novel, written while he lived with them in Hampstead, was about a man who lived in Hampstead with his wife and three children and was writing a novel about it. Furthermore, during the dissolution of Emma's marriage to Robert, possibly before, she takes up with Casey.

The plot of *Betrayal* revolves around the conventional triangle. At a party in 1968, Jerry makes a pass at his friend's wife, who responds. They have an affair and rent a flat. In 1973, Robert learns of it but not only does nothing, he conceals his knowledge from his friend. Two years later (seven years after the affair begins), it ends. In 1977, the marriage does.

The most unusual aspect of *Betrayal* is its dramatic sequence: generally backward in time, accompanied by a sporadic forward movement. Scenes 1 and 2, set in 1977, occur in chronological sequence. Scene 3 takes place in 1975, Scene 4 in 1974. Scenes 5, 6, and 7, set in 1973, occur chronologically. 1971 is the time of Scene 8, 1968 of Scene 9.

Betrayal is somewhat cinematic in nature, since the scenes that do not succeed each other chronologically assume the nature of flashbacks. Like Pinter's screenplays of *Accident* and *The Go-Between*, his *Proust Screenplay* employs flashback. He completed it in 1973, published it in 1977. Thus he corrected its page proofs just before he wrote *Betrayal*, perhaps after he had begun. Unlike his other plays, wherein time past is discussed, *Betrayal* dramatises it. Did Pinter's cinema writings affect it? Considering the number of screenplays he wrote – considering, too, that *The Proust Screenplay* occupied what he calls 'the best working year of my life'[1] – it would be incredible if they did not.

Furthermore, Pinter's view of the work from which *The Proust Screenplay* derives provides a gloss on *Betrayal*. According to him, the structure consists of 'two main and contrasting principles: one, a movement, chiefly narrative, toward disillusion, and the other, more intermittent, toward revelation, rising to where time that was lost is found, and fixed forever in art.' When Proust's Marcel 'says that he is now able to start his work, he has already written it. We have just read it.'[2] In *Betrayal* the backward movement, dramatic not narrative, is toward disillusion; the audience, having witnessed the end of the affair and its aftermath, understands how transitory are the lovers' feelings toward each other during the early time of the affair. The forward movement, more intermittent, is toward such revelations as how the husband deals with his friend after he has discovered his wife's infidelity with him. When the affair is about to begin, the audience has already seen how it ends. Possibly Pinter is more successful in his own work than in his adaptation. It is questionable whether an audience unfamiliar with Proust's original would understand Marcel's statement at the close of the screenplay, 'It was time to begin.'[3] Less questionably, the beginning that ends *Betrayal* is clear, and it fixes in art its retrieval of time lost.

The title is what the play is about, its pervading ambience, what happens in every scene. As one reviewer perceives, betrayal 'resonates more widely than adultery; for Pinter it seems to be the irreducible fact of modern consciousness.'[4]

While the subject of the first scene is the discovery of betrayal (exposition), what happens is also betrayal (dramatic action). At her request, Emma and Jerry meet after their affair is over. Having spent the entire night talking with her husband about the end of their marriage, she says, she suddenly wanted to see Jerry. Her explanation becomes problematic when she states that during her conversation with Robert she confessed she had betrayed him with Jerry – a confession that betrayed Jerry – and when, shortly before, she inquires when Jerry last saw Robert. Not for months, he replies, and questions why she asked. 'I just wondered', she says (15). Unclear at this stage is that she wants to know whether he might have learned earlier what Robert knew. Upon discovering that he probably learned nothing, she provides an explanation to cloak her earlier betrayal when their affair had mattered. To Jerry's surprise she mentions that while they betrayed Robert, he betrayed her with affairs of his own. The scene also suggests, partly because she tries to evade the subject before she denies the charge, that she is having an affair with Casey.

Scene 2, between Robert and Jerry, reveals that Emma lied. She betrayed Jerry by telling her husband of the affair not the night before but four years earlier. Robert betrayed his friendship by hiding his knowledge of this information. According to Robert, Emma may have known of his infidelities. Furthermore both men may be betraying the art to which they have devoted their lives, literature, by promoting Casey, whose books though falling in quality sell well, thereby enriching them.

In Scene 3, the end of the affair, Jerry betrays himself. He refuses to acknowledge that romance is over. When Emma derides the flat by calling it a place 'For fucking', he corrects her: 'No, for loving.' Wryly she points out that little of that is left, but he persists in self-deception: 'I don't think we don't love each other' (55).

In Scene 4, as the audience realises, the husband knows of the affair. By mocking Jerry, he betrays their friendship. For his own amusement he manipulates Jerry into adopting a position he himself states, that boy babies cry more than girl babies, then asks why. When Jerry, off balance, innocently supposes that boy babies are more anxious than girls, Robert makes him defend himself by asking why they should be so anxious at their age. All that occurs to Jerry, who responds in terms established by his cuckolded, seemingly innocent host is that they leave the womb. Robert goads him: 'girl babies [. . .] leave the womb too.' 'That's true. It's also true that nobody talks much about girl babies leaving the womb. Do they?' 'I am prepared to do so' (63–4). The audience's awareness of what will happen permits them to perceive other betrayals as well. In the previous scene, Emma and Jerry reprimand each other for having been unavailable for lovemaking – she too busy in the afternoon, he on a trip to America. In this scene, Jerry disappoints her by announcing he will go to America with Casey – a business necessity that requires betrayal of romance. In retrospect one perceives Emma's betrayal of her values. Whereas she expresses dislike of Casey's writing in this scene, she reverses herself three years later (Scene 1), when she is seeing him. Reverberating throughout Scene 4 are the words 'dishonest' and 'honest', applied not to sex but to squash and writing.

If we recall Scene 2, the announcement that Scene 5

takes place in 1973 alerts us that here Emma will confess her affair with Jerry – a betrayal of her lover (present action) as she reveals betrayal of her husband (past action). Upon confirmation, Robert tries to avenge himself by verbally betraying her: 'I've always liked Jerry. To be honest, I've always liked him more than I've liked you. Maybe I should have had an affair with him myself' (87).

Mel Gussow comments on the differences between Peter Hall's London and New York productions when Robert asks Emma how long the affair has continued. 'Five years', she tells Robert, who responds, '*Five years?*' (86). In London, Penelope Wilton 'was forthcoming about the exposure of the affair, as if to say, "The truth is out; what does it matter?" In contrast, one can feel [Blythe] Danner's [. . .] hesitation about confirming her husband's suspicion.'[5] In the performance of Caroline Lagerfelt, Danner's replacement whom I saw, there was hesitation before she spoke, but her words were neither tentative nor fearful; having decided, during the hesitation, to face the consequences, she spoke forthrightly, her voice slightly betraying fear and guilt. In London, Daniel Massey's response

> provoked explosive laughter. It was as if the time span turned an act of infidelity into a preposterous act of treason. In New York, [Roy] Scheider's reading of the line is a scathing accusation. It is as if he is saying, 'How dare you betray *me* for five years, and with my best friend', not, as in Mr. Massey's version, 'How could I have been so blind?' [. . .] Mr. Scheider adds a feeling of menace to the scene.[6]

When I saw the New York production (twice), well after Gussow did, by which time the actors had settled into their roles, Scheider combined the comic response of the astonished husband (with others in the audience, I laughed – both times), the outrage, and not menace but contained fury.

In Scene 6 Emma betrays Jerry by not revealing that Robert knows. When he casually mentions that he spoke to Robert that morning and will take him to lunch on Thursday, she is nervous. Perhaps sensing something amiss he asks whether she thinks he should not see Robert for lunch on Thursday or any other time. She denies she thinks any such thing.

Scene 7 dramatises the luncheon. Instead of directly confronting Jerry with a confession of his knowledge, Robert does so indirectly, with a parallel confession that connects the same trio and that also involves betrayal – of Robert's former ideals and present profession, book-publishing. In a way that implicates Jerry's professional relationship to him, he lacerates himself, not Jerry: 'I hate books. Or to be more precise, prose. Or to be even more precise, modern prose'; and he contrasts himself (since he had turned down the novel by Jerry's latest discovery, Spinks) with Jerry and Emma (who both admire it): 'You know what you and Emma have in common? You love literature. I mean you love modern prose literature, I mean you love the new novel by the new Casey or Spinks' (115–16).

During Scene 8 the subject of betrayal arises in connection with Jerry's wife, who has an admirer. While she claims there is no more to their relationship than an occasional drink, Emma in time later/scene earlier makes the same claim of herself and Casey. When Emma asks if Jerry thinks his wife is unfaithful, he is uncertain. The love affair is also blighted by Emma's betrayal of Jerry: she confesses that she is pregnant by her husband.

In the final scene the affair begins. Jerry not only betrays his best friend by kissing that friend's wife, she not only betrays her husband by responding, but Pinter reveals – through the hindsight he has dramatised – that the entire affair has consisted of self-betrayal. The inception of their grand passion is merely a pass at a party.

In the London performance by Michael Gambon, says Gussow, 'Jerry was drunk. The pass was almost casual, the emotion offhanded. It was the ultimate irony in an anti-romantic evening.' In the New York performance by Raul Julia, Gussow states, Jerry was 'headstrong. He loves her! [. . .] The evening ends, and the love story begins, with a spark of passion.'[7] In the later performances I saw, Julia did not seem drunk. Emma's accusation of drunkenness thereby became a face-saving device. Nevertheless, Julia was romantic – an interpretation justified by such lines as 'you dazzle me, you jewel, my jewel, I can't ever sleep again' (136). Gambon's performance, as described, harmonises with both the earlier scenes and Pinter's ironic seasonal designations. The end of the marriage takes place in Springtime; the start of the romance, in Winter – a season visualised by the coats on the bed left by party guests.

With the utmost precision, Pinter elegantly links the play's scenes. The first two (Jerry and Emma, then Jerry and Robert) are balanced by the last one (dialogue between Jerry and Emma, then between him and Robert). Afterward the third scene is balanced by the next-to-last, and so forth.

In Scene 1 Jerry and Emma, at a pub, drink light alcoholic beverages; in Scene 9 he may be drunk, she giddy or perhaps high. In Scene 1 he gives her a conventional compliment, 'You're looking very pretty' (18); in Scene 9, a romantic one, 'You're beautiful' (134). An exchange in Scene 1 – 'Darling.' 'Don't say that' (20) – parallels an exchange in Scene 9: 'I love you.' 'My husband is at the other side of that door' (136); but whereas she stops the gambit in Scene 1, she lets him kiss her in Scene 9. In Scene 1 Emma and Jerry discuss the affair; in Scene 9 it begins.

The play's last dialogue echoes Jerry's and Robert's first scene: 'I speak as your oldest friend. Your best man.' 'You are, actually' (138) recalls 'I was your best friend.' 'Well, yes, sure' (39). In Scene 2 Robert tells Jerry the truth (he has known of the affair for four years); in Scene 9 Jerry tells him the truth (he has told Emma how beautiful she was and he is facing the facts). However, Robert faces facts, whereas Jerry disguises fact by overprotestation.

Scenes 3 and 8 take place in the flat. In Scene 3 love is over; in Scene 8 it blooms.

In Scenes 4 and 7 Jerry and Robert are the major figures, another character minor (Emma in 4, the Waiter in 7). Scene 4 begins with Robert pouring a drink for Jerry; Scene 7 has Jerry ordering a drink. In both Jerry is unaware of Robert's knowledge, which Robert uses to taunt him – but with a difference: in Scene 4 Robert mocks only Jerry, in Scene 7 himself as well. In Scene 4 Jerry mentions taking Robert to lunch; in Scene 7 he does so. In Scene 4 Emma cries quietly and briefly; in Scene 7 of the New York production, Roy Scheider quietly and briefly cried, then instantly controlled his show of emotion (the text contains no directive for crying, but Pinter was present, as supervising author, during rehearsals of the New York production).

In Scene 5 Emma is with Robert; in Scene 6, with Jerry. In both, the characters discuss Spinks's novel and Jerry's letter to her. Scene 5 is set in Venice; Scene 6 has her bring to the flat a tablecloth she bought in Venice. In Scene 5 Robert discovers the truth, which Emma confesses; in Scene 6 Jerry fails to discover it and she does not confess; furthermore he relates how his wife almost discovered it – twice. In Scene 5 Robert invites Emma to join him and Jerry for lunch; in Scene 6 she tries to dissuade Jerry from

113

having lunch with Robert.

The echoes are not invariably symmetrical. In Scene 2, for example, Robert reassures Jerry (that it is untrue Jerry did not know much about anything); in Scene 7 Jerry reassures him (that he is not a foolish publisher). In both, the person who has or thinks he has more knowledge is compassionate to his friend.

Betrayal contains Pinter's customary comic devices. When Emma tells her former lover she thought of him the other day, he unexpectedly responds, 'Good God. Why?' (12). Repetition is hilarious, as when Robert recognises that Jerry really did not know he knew of the affair: 'I thought you knew.' 'Knew what?' 'That I knew. That I've known for years. I thought you knew that.' 'You thought I knew?' (38). In the New York production, director and actors inserted a pause and change of focus to stress comic repetition and tautology after Jerry mentions Venice to Robert. An Italian waiter interrupts, 'Venice, signore? Beautiful. A most beautiful place of Italy. You see that painting on the wall?' In production, but not in text, all three turned to look at the cheap reproduction and paused until the waiter explained what needed no explanation, 'Is Venice' (110).

Despite the different dramaturgy of *Betrayal*, it uses familiar techniques and themes. Robert, for example, takes the piss out of Jerry, who is unaware of what lies beneath the surface. Also, consider two statements: 'It's a play about betrayal and distrust'; 'Among many things [it] is about betrayal.' The first is by Pinter on *The Dwarfs*, the second by Paul Rogers on *The Homecoming*.[8] Betrayal is also a theme of other plays by Pinter, including *The Collection* and *The Basement*. Furthermore, the last/chronologically first scene of *Betrayal* can be described in terms of the image Pinter employed for his first play: two people are alone in a room.

In such matters *Betrayal* recapitulates previous plays by Pinter. More important than similarities are major differences. In *Betrayal* Pinter provides what he refused to provide in earlier plays: verification. Also *Betrayal* is his only play in which the audience knows more than the characters do – excepting the first two scenes. *Betrayal* may be his most accessible play since it provides insight into his distinctive techniques. Because we know what happened or what the characters know before it happens or before they know it, we can perceive their manoeuvres as they evade, don masks, and mock each other. When Robert slyly taunts Jerry by asserting his own greater physical fitness, we understand (as Emma does and Jerry does not) his reference to his knowledge of her affair. When he refers to his folly as a publisher, we understand (as Jerry does not) his allusion to his folly as a trusting husband and friend. Because Pinter verifies actions and motivations, we can attend, without bafflement about the past, to the dramatic present.

Although Pinter has been writing plays for almost a quarter of a century, it seems likely from these recent works that his inventiveness is far from exhausted. To the contrary, he appears to be renewing himself, finding fresh areas and means to express his changing dramatic vision. Extending himself, he also maintains his footing on familiar terrain. His fresh starts are from fixed points, which provide solid technical bases for his dramatic departures. What the unmasked face of *Monologue*, the personal subject of *No Man's Land*, or the major dramaturgical departure of *Betrayal* may forecast is impossible to predict. One looks forward to the next Pinter play with the same eagerness one did ten or twenty years ago. A comparable statement can be made of few other contemporary dramatists.

8
The Place of Pinter

Unlike such dramatists as Arthur Miller, Harold Pinter dislikes talking about his own work. 'I'm a writer, not a critic', he says. When pressed he prefers to discuss practical matters, but he admits that this preference is 'no more than a pious hope, since one invariably slips into theorising, almost without noticing it, and I distrust theory.'[1] Nevertheless his theoretical statements are acute. Like the minimalist dialogue of his plays, his minimalist theorising resonates widely.

'I *am* a very traditional playwright', he says, as preparation for two gags: 'for instance I insist on having a curtain in all my plays' (very traditional, this, in our era of thrust stages and aprons that extend beyond curtainless proscenium arches to cover orchestra pits) and 'I write curtain lines for that reason!'[2] Part of the jokes' effectiveness lies in so unconventional a dramatist calling himself traditional. Paradoxically, however, he is, and his traditionalism consists of more than an inclination to write curtain lines (i.e., powerful speeches at the end of acts, to herald the closing of the curtain) for stage plays that employ a conventional box

116

set within a curtained proscenium arch. For that matter he does not so confine himself when he writes plays in other dramatic media or when he has at his disposal, as he did when he wrote *Betrayal*, a stage with the technical resources of the National Theatre's Lyttleton. Despite Pinter's distinctive dramaturgy, which the first chapter in particular has noted, his writings, as that chapter has also noted, have links to the Theatre of the Absurd and to the realism of such mid-century dramatists as John Osborne. Furthermore they are part of an older tradition of English drama and of modern European drama in general.

Although Pinter has not consciously looked to any particular dramatist for guidance, he admits his longstanding admiration of Samuel Beckett and comments, sensibly, 'You don't write in a vacuum; you're bound to absorb and digest other writing; and I admire Beckett's work so much that something of its texture might appear in my own. I myself have no idea whether this is so, but if it is, then I am grateful for it.'[3] In an early study of Pinter, Ruby Cohn juxtaposes excerpts of *Waiting for Godot* and *The Birthday Party*. Beckett's play contains an exchange between Vladimir and Estragon about Godot's reply to a question of theirs:

> That he'd see.
> That he couldn't promise anything.
> That he'd have to think it over.
> In the quiet of his home.
> Consult his family.
> His friends.
> His agents.
> His correspondents.
> His books.
> His bank accounts.

In Pinter's play, Goldberg and McCann promise Stanley:

> You'll be integrated.
> You'll give orders.
> You'll make decisions.
> You'll be a magnate.
> A statesman.
> You'll own yachts.
> Animals' (I,94).

While Beckett's tramps 'still attempt to define the System in familiar human terms', Pinter's messengers 'glibly mouth its pat phrases'. Yet both dramatists employ 'pithy stichomythia'.[4] Though (in this passage) Beckett's characters also mouth pat phrases, they talk as outsiders, whereas Pinter's act as spokesmen. Each play shapes its own distinctive dialogue, but as Cohn perceives, Pinter's 'pithy stichomythia' recalls Beckett's.

Kenneth Tynan may have been the first to cite T. S. Eliot as one of Pinter's literary progenitors, and he compared the 'lurking violence' and the repetitive dialogue of *The Dumb Waiter* ('When he sees you behind him –' 'Me behind him –' 'And me in front of him –' 'And you in front of him –' (I,160)) with those of *Sweeney Agonistes* ('What did he do?/ All the time, what did he do?'/'What did he do! What did he do?').[5] Pinter may or may not have been familiar with these unfinished fragments, as Eliot subtitles the two scenes of *Sweeney Agonistes*, but an actor of his generation could hardly have been unfamiliar with Eliot's *The Cocktail Party*. The light banter between Julia and Peter – 'He was very clever at repairing clocks;/And he had a remarkable sense of hearing –/The only man I ever met who could hear the cry of bats.'/'Hear the cry of bats?' 'He could hear the cry of bats.'/'How do you know he could hear the cry of bats?'/'Because he said so. And I believed him'[6] – seems to be echoed by such passages as Bill's and James's in *The Collection*:

> Yes, he's very good at parties. Bit of a conjurer.
> What, rabbits?
> Well, not so much rabbits, no.
> No rabbits?
> No. He doesn't like rabbits, actually. They give him hay fever.
> Poor chap (II,134).

While neither pithy nor stichomythic, the dialogue rhythms of Pinter's prose recall those of Eliot's verse.

In the same article Tynan also mentioned Pinter's indebtedness to Noel Coward – to whom, one should add, the Eliot of *The Cocktail Party* is also indebted. Coward, too, is a playwright whose major works an actor of Pinter's generation was apt to be familiar with. In the typical and popular *Private Lives* Coward has dialogue between the honeymooning Sybil and Elyot:

> Oh dear, I'm so happy.
> Are you?
> Aren't you?
> Of course I am. Tremendously happy.
> Just to think, here we are you and I, married!
> Yes, things have come to a pretty pass.
> Don't laugh at me, you mustn't be *blasé* about honeymoons just because this is your second.[7]

Tea Party also contains a honeymoon scene, also the second honeymoon for the man, with dialogue between Disson and Diana:

Are you happy?
Yes.'
Very happy?
Yes.'
Have you ever been happier? With any other man?
Never.
I make you happy, don't I? Happier than you've ever
been . . . with any other man.
Yes. You do (III,120).

Each playwright puts his banter to different use. Coward's
woman requires reassurance from the man, whereas Pinter's man requires it from the woman. Nevertheless it
seems clear that however coincidental the dramatists' subject matter may be, their technique of parallel rhythms and
repetitions links them in the same comic tradition.

In terms of comic drama, Bernard Shaw is a progenitor of
both. While neither their plays nor Eliot's (nor Somerset
Maugham's nor Terence Rattigan's; the list could of course
be longer) share the social vision of Shaw's, they do share
comic techniques, including rhythm and repetition. One
Pinter-like Shavian example is an exchange among Pothi-
nus, Caesar, and Rufio in *Caesar and Cleopatra*: 'Caesar: I
come to warn you of a danger, and to make you an offer.'
'Never mind the danger. Make the offer.' 'Never mind the
offer. Whats the danger?'[8] For passages that resemble each
other, like those just cited, compare Boss Mangan and Ellie
Dunn in *Heartbreak House* – 'Youre not in earnest?' 'Yes I
am. Arnt you?' 'You mean to hold me to it?' 'Do you wish
to back out of it?'[9] – with Spooner and Hirst in *No Man's
Land:* 'when we had our cottage . . . we gave our visitors
tea, on the lawn.' 'I did the same.' 'On the lawn?' 'I did the
same.' 'You had a cottage?' 'Tea on the lawn' (28–9). Ironically it is the terse Pinter who repeats exactly the same

phrases, whereas the supposedly garrulous Shaw, in the shorter passage, varies them. Their dramatic stratagems differ. Whereas Shaw's dialogue is dialectical, thereby prompting change, Pinter's dialogue reflects unyielding characters who rigidly refuse to give way. Despite taut rhythm and comic repetition, Shaw's characters are quick to explain, as in this exchange between Sarah and Lomax in *Major Barbara*: 'Cholly: we're going to the works this afternoon.' 'What works?' 'The cannon works.'[10] Some of Pinter's characters are either unwilling to explain or are incapable of doing so. Therefore, as in this exchange between Lenny and Joey in *The Homecoming*, they provide repetition in lieu of explanation: 'Tell him about the last bird you had, Joey.' 'What bird?' 'The last bird!' (III,82–3).

As these quotations demonstrate, Pinter is part of an English tradition of comic dialogue that includes the anglicised Irish Shaw, the anglicised American Eliot, and the gallicised Irish Beckett. It does not follow, however, that all playwrights who are part of this tradition write in the same manner. As Cohn says of Beckett and Pinter, they do not, despite their commonality. Nor does it follow that each dramatist writes the same way in every play. They do not. Their language changes to conform to character, situation, and theme.

Demonstrating this change are the varied ways in which Pinter's characters employ epithets to denigrate each other. In *The Collection* James calls the sophisticated Bill old-fashioned names: 'You're a wag, aren't you?' and 'I bet you're a wow at parties' (II,133–4). In *No Man's Land* young Foster addresses old Spooner with boyish names: 'Hey, scout' and 'Listen, chummeybum' (48–9). Different characters employ different sentimental clichés to describe their late wives. In *The Birthday Party* Goldberg recollects a wife in warmly maternal terms: 'I had a wife. What a wife.

[. . .] "Simey", my wife used to shout, "quick, before it gets cold!" And there on the table what would I see? The nicest piece of rollmop and pickled cucumber you could wish to find on a plate' (I,69). In *The Homecoming* Max recalls a mother in terms of frigid pedagogy, with heart as a mocking byproduct:

> If only your mother was alive. [. . .] Mind you, she taught those boys everything they know. She taught them all the morality they know: I'm telling you. Every single bit of the moral code they live by – was taught to them by their mother. And she had a heart to go with it. What a heart (III,61–2).

Even when characters use the same initial phrase, the situation determines what follows. In *The Birthday Party* it is the security of the expected and familiar: 'Is that you, Petey? Petey, is that you? Petey?' 'What?' 'Is that you?' 'Yes, it's me.' 'What?' (I,19). In *The Collection* it is the insecurity of the unexpected and unfamiliar: 'Is that you, Bill?' 'Yes?' 'Are you in?' 'Who's this?' (II,125).

Pinter's dialogue, which forms an integral part of his dramatic technique, has an indirect, tangential quality comparable to that of August Strindberg and Anton Chekhov, who are among the founders of modern European drama. In the 1888 Preface to *Miss Julie* Strindberg articulated the naturalistic nature of dialogue and character. In this play characters are not 'interlocutors who ask stupid questions to elicit witty answers'. The play avoids 'the symmetrical and mathematical design of the artfully constructed French dialogue' of the well-made play but lets the characters' minds 'work as irregularly as they do in real life, where no subject is quite exhausted before another mind engages at random some cog in the conversation and governs it for a while'. The dialogue therefore wanders, and it 'gathers material in the first scenes which is later picked up, repeated, reworked, developed, and expanded like the theme in a piece of music.'[11] This famous theoretical work and the more famous play it introduces were available to Pinter when he was a young acting student and professional actor; though he may not have read the Preface, he was not likely to have missed the play, whose dialogue the Preface accurately characterises, and characterises Pinter's as well. Pinter was less likely to have read a letter by Chekhov, written the same year as Strindberg's work: 'The business of a writer of fiction is only to describe who it was that talked or thought about God or pessimism, how they did it, and under what circumstances. An artist is [. . .] only an impartial witness.'[12] Yet he was apt to have read or seen one of Chekhov's four major plays, whose dialogue conforms to what Chekhov said a fictionist should write. Perhaps because Pinter's writing resembles Chekhov's in this respect, one of his theoretical statements resembles the quoted passage by Chekhov: 'Given characters who possess a momentum of their own, my job is not to impose upon them, not to subject them to a false articulation, by which I mean forcing a character to speak where he could not speak, making him speak in a way he could not speak, or making him speak of what he could never speak' (I,14). For all Pinter's elliptical stylisation, his dialogue conforms to this naturalistic tradition, in which characters speak for themselves, in as apparently rambling and tangential ways as they would in real life, and do not speak with false articulation for a partial author.

The naturalistic tradition includes social verisimilitude. Though not obviously so, Pinter's plays contain as much verisimilitude of this type as the plays of John Osborne and Arthur Miller. His characters inhabit a socially recognisable milieu. If early critics stress this milieu, the reason is not that they are accustomed to such drama and are insufficiently alert to Pinter's distinctive idiom. Rather, social reality is a vital part of Pinter's plays, more clearly in the earlier than in the later works. To Pinter, fear of unspecified menace from outside one's sheltering room, fear that the balance upon which one's life is perched may be upset, is neither unrealistic nor surrealistic. He grew up during World War II when the Nazis overran Europe and for a time seemed likely to overrun England herself, and he wrote his first plays during the post-Atomic era when nuclear holocaust was a realistic not a paranoiac threat, which it may still be. As he said in 1960, 'this thing, of people arriving at the door, has been happening in Europe in the last twenty years. Not only the last twenty years, the last two to three hundred.'[13] Pinter's outlook is sensitive to the society of which he is a part.

Unlike a number of his contemporaries, who also write in the tradition of realism or naturalism, Pinter refuses to turn his stage into a political platform. 'Ultimately, politics do bore me', he says, but he also says:

> I'll tell you what I really think about politicians. The other night I watched some politicians on television talking about [the war in] Vietnam. I wanted very much to burst through the screen with a flamethrower and burn their eyes out and their balls off and then inquire from them how they would assess this action from a political point of view.

The person who wanted to do this is someone who, notwithstanding the first assertion, is angered rather than bored by politics. The latter type of person would probably not bother to watch that television programme. When Pinter says he finds politics tedious, he may mean useless as a basis for his art, which concerns people who either are uninterested in politics or else are in situations wherein the subject does not arise. Supporting this inference is Pinter's statement, in the same interview that furnishes these quotations, 'I don't like being subjected to propaganda, and I detest soapboxes. [. . .] The chasm between the war in Vietnam' and a stage presentation of it is 'so enormous as to be quite preposterous. [. . .] It's impossible to make a major theatrical statement about such a matter when television and the press have made everything so clear.'[14] The reasons he admires Samuel Beckett, as he wrote to a friend in 1954 – though he forgot the letter until the friend showed it to him a dozen years later – include qualities, or rather the absence of qualities, whose absence also distinguishes his own drama: 'I don't want philosophies, tracts, dogmas, creeds, way outs, truths, answers, *nothing from the bargain basement.* [. . .] he's not flogging me a remedy or a path or a revelation [. . .] *he hasn't got his hand over his heart.*'[15]

However, this is not to say that Pinter is apolitical. The man who, at the risk of imprisonment, twice refused to enter the armed forces is not a man with no commitment to social ideas (his statement about Vietnam suggests a commitment against that war). Goldberg's platitudes reveal much about the conformist mould of middle-class Englishmen. Davies's racial and national animosities may say a great deal about the psychological outlet of a repressed, downtrodden, and mal-educated or uneducated member of the lower classes, as may his awe at Mick's trite decorating ideas Lenny's mockery of the fact that his brother is a professor in an American university may ultimately show as much about social attitudes as a play clearly about the class structure. Disson's revelation of his lower-class origins and his insecurity with his higher-class wife and her brother may be similarly revealing. The declassment portrayed in *No Man's Land* emerges in diction, not as the subject of conversation. Pinter's characters do not discuss such subjects as wars, politics, race relations, economics, or unemployment, but such subjects influence their attitudes, actions, and diction; and they occasionally, though briefly, surface as themes: a reference to blacks (*The Caretaker*) or to profitmaking (*Betrayal*), for example. To refuse to write discursive plays about social awareness is not to be socially or politically ignorant, or to live in a social vacuum. Pinter is not and does not. Whereas 'the ordinary dramatist only neglects social questions because he knows nothing about them', as Bernard Shaw said in 1895, 'With the great dramatic poet it is otherwise.' The latter devours 'everything with a keen appetite – fiction, science, gossip, politics, technical processes, sport, everything'; and he comprehends all sectarian strains.[16] Pinter's drama is a product of that appetite, and it comprehends and non-discursively reflects the world around it.

But Pinter is not unqualifiedly naturalistic. His statement about his writing, 'The more acute the experience the less articulate its expression' (I,11), brings to mind the words of Maurice Maeterlinck, who in 1896 lamented that, in the theatre of his day, he would 'almost invariably' meet a character 'who would tell me, at wearisome length, why he was jealous, why he poisoned, or why he killed. [. . .] I have grown to believe that an old man, seated in his armchair, [...] motionless as he is, does yet live in reality a deeper, more human and more universal life.'[17] Maeterlinck's description of what he calls static drama, which he advocates, seems also to describe many of Pinter's plays, notably *Landscape*. Perhaps Pinter comes to Maeterlinck, if he does come to him, by way of Beckett, perhaps by way of W. B. Yeats, to whom characters in *Betrayal* refer. Contrasting impassioned, poetic drama with the prose drama of city people, Yeats described, in 1896, a type of writer and a type of play much like Pinter and his drama, written more than half a century later. The best writers of the latter type of play 'keep to the surface, never showing anything but the arguments and the persiflage of daily observation, or now and then, instead of the expression of passion, a stage picture, a man holding a woman's hand or sitting with his head in dim light by the red glow of a fire'.[18] Such surface-of-life arguments and persiflage, and such stage pictures, rather than direct expressions of passion, characterise plays like *The Caretaker* (the discourse between Davies and Aston; the stage picture of Aston by the window, his back toward Davies, on whom the lighting fades), *The Collection* (the arguments and persiflage of James and Bill; the picture of Stella, smiling and silently stroking a cat while her husband awaits confirmation), and *The Homecoming* (the initial encounter of Teddy and Lenny; the stage picture of Ruth seated, two men on their knees by her, another standing apart from them).

The utmost precision marks his stage craftsmanship. The very fact that he distinguishes among three dots, pauses, and silences to suggest varying durations of non-speech should suggest as much. So should his comments on dramatic structure, which are consistent, for instance: 'I pay meticulous attention to the shape of things, from the shape of a sentence to the overall structure of the play. This shaping, to put it mildly, is of the first importance' (I,14) and 'that's my main concern, to get the structure right [. . .] For me everything has to do with shape, structure, and overall unity'.[19] As mentioned previously, characters in *The Dumb Waiter* respond at the beginning and end of the play to newspaper stories, and front-to-back scenes of *Betrayal* mirror each other. The shape and structure of most of Pinter's plays reflect his distinctive type of tragicomedy, suggested by his statements that everything, even tragedy, is funny, until the play reaches a point where it is no longer funny, and that *The Caretaker* is funny up to a point, beyond which it stops being funny. Initially Pinter's tragicomedy establishes comic terms but it moves toward a point where what was comic is no longer comic, and then it denies the exclusiveness of the attributes of the comic genre it primarily establishes, the type of change and conclusion associated with comedy (the happy ending), and the response comedy normally evokes. Furthermore, from that point on, the sources of the noncomic are the same as those of the comic even while they deny the exclusiveness of comic attributes.[20]

Critical recognition as one of today's major dramatists came relatively quickly to Harold Pinter. In 1958 the English press – with one notable exception, the frequently prescient Harold Hobson – rejected him. Within a mere two years, however, they acclaimed him, and even then journalistic critics recognised that, despite his distinctiveness, he was part of a dramatic tradition that included Beckett, Eliot, and Coward. By this time, too, academic critics began to perceive his importance. In the early 1960s prudence tempered praise, for Pinter was young and his output small. Before the decade was over, though he was still relatively young and his dramatic corpus only somewhat larger, most critics, both journalistic and academic, proclaimed him as pre-eminent among contemporary playwrights, and 1970 saw the publication of the first book-length study of Pinter by another usually prescient critic, Martin Esslin, who was among the first to recognise his abilities. In fact Esslin's contribution was more than critical. As head of BBC radio drama he was responsible for commissioning Pinter to write *A Slight Ache* – shortly after the failure of *The Birthday Party* and well before the success of *The Caretaker*.

Today it is commonplace to call Pinter one of the best living dramatists who write in the English language – or in any language. His position is secure. He has been flattered by imitators, none of whom rivals him. In more than twenty years of playwriting he has demonstrated his stature. As a dramatist he has grown considerably, refusing to confine himself to a single mould. The five plays that the last five chapters treat at length demonstrate this refusal. For Pinter repetition is a dramatic technique but infrequently a playwriting habit. The affinities of *The Birthday Party* and *The Caretaker* to *The Homecoming* and *Old Times*, or of all to *Betrayal*, testify to a distinctive artistic signature, but each play differs substantially from the others in focus and form. Within the parameters of his art, Pinter's writing demonstrates remarkable variety as well as remarkable quality. The critical commonplace that begins this paragraph is uncommon critical sense: Pinter *is* among the most important dramatists now living.

References

Unless specified here, fuller publication details will be found in the Bibliography.

1. Introduction

1. 20 May 1958, in Martin Esslin, *Pinter: A Study of his Plays* (1973), p. 18.
2. G. Wilson Knight, 'The Kitchen Sink', *Encounter* 21 (Dec. 1963), pp. 48–9.
3. Martin Esslin, *The Theatre of the Absurd* (1969), pp. 5–6.
4. E.g., Knight, 51; Laurence Kitchen, *Mid-Century Drama* (1960), p. 114.
5. Lawrence M. Bensky, 'Harold Pinter: An Interview', *The Paris Review*, 10 Autumn 1966) 19–20.
6. Peter Hall, 'Directing Pinter', *Theatre Quarterly*, 4 (Nov. 1974–Jan. 1975), 4–17.
7. Katherine H. Burkman, *The Dramatic World of Harold Pinter* (1971), p. 121.
8. Mel Gussow, 'A Conversation (Pause) with Harold Pinter', *The New York Times Magazine* (5 Dec. 1971) 134.
9. Stephen Watts, 'Rattigan's Image', *The New York Times* (10 Nov. 1963), 26.
10. Samuel Beckett, 'Dante . . . Bruno. Vico . . Joyce', *Our Exagmination. . .* (1962) p. 14.

11. Gussow, 43.
12. Hall, 10.
13. John Russell Taylor, 'Accident', *Sight and Sound*, 35 (Autumn 1966) 184.
14. *Daily Mail*, 28 November 1967, in Esslin, *Pinter*, pp. 37–8.

2. Biographical Survey

1. Bensky, 'Harold Pinter', 31.
2. Kenneth Tynan, *Show People* (1979) pp. 50–3.
3. Mel Gussow, 'Harold Pinter: "I Started with Two People in a Pub"', *The New York Times* (30 Dec. 1979) 8.
4. Esslin, *Pinter*, pp. 19–20.
5. Hall, 'Directing Pinter', 14.
6. The chronology at the start of each volumne of Pinter's *Complete Works* gives 1966 as year of writing. In discussing the play later, however, I use 1963 as year of original composition and place it between *The Lover* and *Tea Party*.
7. Bensky, 14.
8. 'Pinter Marriage', *The Times*, 10 October 1980, 2.
9. In analysing the play, I place it at the time of composition, 1958, between *The Dumb Waiter* and *A Slight Ache*.

3. Menace and the Absurd

1. Irving Wardle, 'There's Music in That Room', *Encore*, 7 (July–Aug. 1960), 33.
2. Bensky, 'Harold Pinter', 23.
3. For these perceptions, I am grateful to Wayne Babineau.
4. Steven H. Gale, *Butter's Going Up: A Critical Analysis of Harold Pinter's Work* (1977), p. 37.
5. Gale offers both interpretations: ibid., pp. 48–9.
6. Glynne Wickham, *Drama in a World of Science* (1962), pp. 28–9.
7. Austin E. Quigley, *The Pinter Problem* (1975) pp. 64–5.
8. Bensky, 28–9.
9. William Baker and Stephen Ely Tabachnick, *Harold Pinter* (1973) p. 37.

4. Toward Greater Realism

1. Quigley, *The Pinter Problem*, p. 150.
2. Esslin, *Pinter*, p. 51. For a fuller application of this idea, see Bernard F. Dukore, *Where Laughter Stops: Pinter's Tragicomedy* (1976).
3. Esslin, *Pinter*, p. 113.

5. Struggles For Power

1. Quigley, *The Pinter Problem*, pp. 55–6.
2. Hall, 'Directing Pinter', 6.
3. Ibid., 9.
4. Peter Hall, 'A Director's Approach', in John Lahr (ed.), *A Casebook on Harold Pinter's 'The Homecoming'*, p. 20; Paul Rogers, 'An Actor's Approach', ibid., p. 169.
5. Henry Hewes, 'Probing Pinter's Play', *Saturday Review*, 50 (8 Apr. 1967) 58.
6. Rogers, p. 165; John Normington, 'An Actor's Approach', ibid., pp. 140–1.
7. Richard Hornby, *Script into Performance* (1977) pp. 179–80.

6. Memory Plays

1. Harold Pinter, *Five Screenplays* (1971, 1973) p. 287.

7. Recapitulations and Fresh Starts

1. Harold Pinter, *The Proust Screenplay* (1977) p. x.
2. Ibid., pp. ix–x.
3. Ibid., p. 177. Noel King also connects the final line of *The Proust Screenplay* to *Betrayal*. See his 'Pinter's Progress', *Modern Drama,* 23 (Sept. 1980), 256. This issue reached me in mid-November 1980, well after I had completed this book.
4. Jack Kroll, 'Pinter's Dance of Deception', *Newsweek*, 95 (21 Jan. 1980), 86. From a different viewpoint, Linda Ben-Zui explores types of betrayal in this play. See her 'Harold Pinter's *Betrayal*: The Patterns of Banality', *Modern Drama*, 23 (Sept. 1980), 228–35. As indicated in note 3 above, I received this issue well after completion of this book.
5. Mel Gussow, 'London to Broadway: How a Culture Shapes a Show' *The New York Times* (3 Feb. 1980), 35.
6. Ibid.
7. Ibid.
8. Bensky, 'Harold Pinter', 23; Hewes, 'Probing Pinter's Play', p. 56.

8. The Place of Pinter

1. Harold Pinter, 'Pinter on Pinter', *Cinebill*, 1 (Oct. 1973) 5.
2. Bensky, 'Harold Pinter', 36.
3. Harry Thompson, 'Harold Pinter Replies', *New Theatre Magazine*, 2 (Jan. 1961) 8–9.

References

4.   Ruby Cohn, 'The World of Harold Pinter', *Tulane Drama Review*, 6 (March 1962) 59. The Beckett passage cited (longer in Cohn's article) is in *Waiting for Godot*, pp. 40–40a.

5.   Kenneth Tynan, *Tynan Right and Left* (1968) p. 76. The passage cited is in T. S. Eliot, *The Complete Plays and Poems 1909–1950* (1952) p. 83. Both quotations are longer in Tynan's article.

6.   Eliot, p. 299.

7.   Noel Coward, *Play Parade* (1933) pp. 183–4.

8.   Bernard Shaw, *The Bodley Head Bernard Shaw: Collected Plays with Their Prefaces* (1971–2) vol. 2, p. 263. Shavian quotations reproduce his idiosyncratic punctuation and spelling.

9.   Ibid., vol. 5, p. 110.

10.   Ibid., vol. 3, p. 141.

11.   August Strindberg, 'Preface to *Miss Julie*', trans. Evert Sprinchorn, in Bernard F. Dukore (ed.), *Dramatic Theory and Criticism: Greeks to Grotowski* (1974) p. 570.

12.   Letter to A. S. Suvorin, trans. D. C. Gerould, ibid., p. 913.

13.   Esslin, *Pinter*, p. 36.

14.   Bensky, 28, 33.

15.   Harold Pinter, 'Beckett', *Beckett at Sixty: A Festschrift* (1967) p. 86. Italics are his.

16.   Bernard Shaw, 'The Problem Play', in Dukore, *Dramatic Theory*, p. 633.

17.   Maurice Maeterlinck, 'The Tragical in Daily Life', trans. Alfred Sutro, ibid., pp. 728–9.

18.   W. B. Yeats, *Essays and Introductions*, pp. 274–5.

19.   Bensky, 26, 37.

20.   See Dukore, *Where Laughter Stops*, pp. 4–5 and *passim*.

Bibliography

(i) Writings by Pinter

'Beckett', *Beckett at Sixty: A Festschrift* (London: Calder and Boyars, 1967).

Betrayal (London: Eyre Methuen, 1978; New York: Grove Press, 1979).

Complete Works, 3 vols (London: Eyre Methuen; New York, Grove Press, 1977—8).

Five Screenplays (London: Eyre Methuen, 1971; New York: Grove Press, 1973).

The Hothouse (London: Eyre Methuen, 1980.

Monologue (London: Covent Garden Press, 1973).

No Man's Land (London: Eyre Methuen; New York: Grove Press, 1975).

Old Times (London: Eyre Methuen; New York: Grove Press, 1971).

'Pinter on Pinter', *Cinebill,* 1 (Oct. 1973), 5—7. American Film Theatre Programme, *The Homecoming.*

Poems and Prose 1949—1977 (London: Eyre Methuen; New York: Grove Press. 1978).

The Proust Screenplay (London: Eyre Methuen; New York: Grove Press, 1977).

(ii) Selected Secondary Sources

Baker, William and Stephen Ely Tabachnick, *Harold Pinter* (Edinburgh: Oliver and Boyd, 1973).

Bibliography

Beckett, Samuel, 'Dante . . .Bruno. Vico . . Joyce.', *Our Examination Round His Factification for Incamination of Work in Progress* (New York: Grove Press, 1962).

_____, *Waiting for Godot* (New York: Grove Press, 1954).

Ben-Zvi, Linda, 'Harold Pinter's *Betrayal*: The Patterns of Banality', *Modern Drama*, 23 (Sept. 1980) 227–37.

Bensky, Lawrence M., 'Harold Pinter: An Interview', *The Paris Review*, 10 (Fall 1966) 13–37.

Burkman, Katherine H., *The Dramatic World of Harold Pinter: Its Basis in Ritual* (Columbus: Ohio State University Press, 1971).

Cohn, Ruby, 'The World of Harold Pinter', *Tulane Drama Review*, 6 (March 1962) 55–68.

Coward, Noel, *Play Parade* (Garden City, N.Y.: Doubleday, Doran, 1933).

Dukore, Bernard F., *Where Laughter Stops: Pinter's Tragicomedy* (Columbia: University of Missouri Press, 1976).

_____(ed.), *Dramatic Theory and Criticism: Greeks to Grotowski* (New York: Holt, Rinehart and Winston, 1974).

Eliot, T. S., *The Complete Plays and Poems 1909–1950* (New York: Harcourt, Brace and World, 1952).

Esslin, Martin, *Pinter: A Study of His Plays* (London: Eyre Methuen, 1973).

_____, *The Theatre of the Absurd* (Garden City, N.Y.: Doubleday, 1969).

Gale, Steven H., *Butter's Going Up: A Critical Analysis of Harold Pinter's Work* (Durham, N.C.: Duke University Press, 1977).

Ganz, Arthur (ed.), *Pinter* (Englewood Cliffs, N.J.: Prentice-Hall, 1972).

Gussow, Mel, 'A Conversation (Pause) with Harold Pinter', *The New York Times Magazine* (5 Dec. 1971) 42–3, 126–36.

_____, 'Harold Pinter: "I started with Two People in a Pub"', *The New York Times* (30 Dec. 1979) sec. 2: 5, 7–8.

_____, 'London to Broadway: How a Culture Shapes a Show', *The New York Times* (3 Feb. 1980) sec. 2: 1, 2, 35.

Hall, Peter, 'Directing Pinter', *Theatre Quarterly*, 4 (Nov. 1974 – Jan. 1975) 4–17.

Hewes, Henry, 'Probing Pinter's Play', *Saturday Review*, 50 (8 Apr. 1967) 56, 58, 96–7.

Hornby, Richard, *Script into Performance* (Austin: University of Texas Press, 1977).

Kennedy, Andrew, *Six Dramatists in Search of a Language* (Cambridge: Cambridge University Press, 1975).

King, Noel, 'Pinter's Progress', *Modern Drama*, 23 (Sept. 1980) 246–57.

Kitchin, Lawrence, *Mid-Century Drama* (London: Faber and Faber, 1960).

Knight, G. Wilson, 'The Kitchen Sink', *Encounter*, 21 (Dec. 1963), 48–54.

Bibliography

Kroll, Jack, 'Pinter's Dance of Deception', *Newsweek*, 95 (21 Jan. 1980) 86.

Lahr, John (ed.), *A Casebook on Harold Pinter's 'The Homecoming'* (New York: Grove Press, 1971).

Modern Drama, 17 (Dec. 1974) Harold Pinter issue.

Quigley, Austin E., *The Pinter Problem* (Princeton, N.J.: Princeton University Press, 1975).

Shaw, Bernard, *The Bodley Head Bernard Shaw: Collected Plays with Their Prefaces*, vols. 2, 3, 5 (London: The Bodley Head, 1971–72).

Taylor, John Russell, 'Accident', *Sight and Sound*, 35 (Autumn 1966) 179–84.

_____, *Anger and After* (Baltimore: Penguin Books, 1963).

Thompson, Harry, 'Harold Pinter Replies', *New Theatre Magazine*, 2 (Jan. 1961) 8–10.

Tynan, Kenneth, *Show People* (New York: Simon and Schuster, 1979).

_____, *Tynan Right and Left* (New York: Atheneum, 1968).

Wardle, Irving, 'There's Music in That Room', *Encore*, 7 (July–Aug. 1960) 32–4.

Watts, Stephen, 'Rattigan's Image', *The New York Times* (10 Nov. 1963) 26.

Wickham, Glynne, *Drama in a World of Science* (London: Routledge and Kegan Paul, 1962).

Yeats, W. B., *Essays and Introductions* (New York: Macmillan, 1961).

Index

Index

Index